Envisioning Architecture

An Analysis of Drawing

Iain Fraser
Rod Henmi

Supported by a grant from the Graham Foundation for Advanced Studies in the Fine Arts.

JOHN WILEY & SONS, INC.

New York Chichester Weinheim Brisbane Singapore Toronto

This publication is designed to provide accurate and authoritative information in regard to the subject matter covered. It is sold with the understanding that the publisher is not engaged in rendering professional services. If professional advice or other expert assistance is required, the services of a competent professional person should be sought.

Library of Congress Cataloging-in-Publication Data:

15 14 13 12 11

Fraser, Iain.
    Envisioning architecture: an analysis of drawing / Iain Fraser,
Rod Henmi.
        p. cm.
    ISBN 0-471-28479-3
    1. Architectural drawing.   I. Henmi, Rod.   II. Title.
NA2700.F73   1993
    720'.28'4—dc20   92-34491
                                                                 CIP

Printed in the United States of America

Contents

Acknowledgments   v

Preface   vii

1 The Lessons of Drawing for Le Corbusier   1

Section 1 Drawing Types   23

2 Orthographic Drawings   25

3 Axonometric Drawings   45

4 Perspective Drawings   58

Section 2 Applications of Drawing   81

5 Referential Drawings   83

6 Diagrams   99

7 Design Drawings   113

8 Presentation Drawings   131

9 Visionary Drawings   147

10 Representation   161

Endnotes   171

Bibliography   179

Index   189

Acknowledgments

We would like to thank the School of Architecture at Washington University, and especially Dean Constantine Michaelides, for continuing support and encouragement. We are grateful for financial support received from the Graham Foundation for Advanced Studies in the Fine Arts and for material support contributed by The Harris Armstrong Foundation. Andy Bernheimer with the assistance of Andy Bonnano contributed significant logistical help. Our thanks also go to Kathleen O'Donnell and Bobbe Winters for their unstinting efforts throughout the long period of preparation and production.

We received important critical advice from Professor Carl Safe and are especially grateful to Professor Rob Jensen for his continuous encouragement, critical acumen and helpful insight into the project. We acknowledge with gratitude the efforts made by those who helped provide reproductions from their respective archives, foundations, and collections. We extend our deep appreciation to all of the individuals who contributed their drawings and good will, with special consideration to James Stirling who offered insight and support prior to his untimely passing.

Finally, to the following we would like to dedicate this book.

By Iain Fraser:
To my daughters, Jessica and Madeline.

By Rod Henmi:
To my family, in memory of my mother.

Preface

The phenomenon of drawing lies prominently between the imagination of the architect and the design of a building. It is an activity at once highly conventionalized and very personal, shared but private, involving the discovery of forms, their communication both internally and externally, and the resolution of three-dimensional complexities through a two-dimensional format. Drawing reveals, edits, persuades, highlights, and sometimes obscures. Necessary for the making of architecture (as buildings are almost always drawn in some way), its techniques are exhaustively taught in architectural schools—its products widely published. The culture of drawing is a continuous, ongoing activity. Drawings are ubiquitous and persistent presences in the domain of architecture. Yet it is this commonness, this everyday aspect, that prevents one from seeing drawing itself. That is, drawing is so pervasive in the field of architecture that it is sometimes difficult to get a clear view of its effects. The awareness of its impact is submerged by the weight and pure volume of drawings. It seems so natural, so inherently necessary, that to ask such questions as the following seems almost too obvious: What is drawing? What are its effects? What role does it play in the making of architecture? How has drawing been used? What impact might different drawing constructs have on the methods and results of design?

When a medium such as drawing is held so intimately and used so frequently, it is often difficult to gain a more distant view, a more conscious awareness. Although designers are very familiar with drawings, with their tones and textures, and with many examples by noted practitioners, they may still be unaware of exactly how those drawings fit into the working methods of those architects and how their technique influenced thought. This book analyzes drawings within the context of design, showing a wide range of types and applications by a variety of architects, allowing for focused consideration and increased understanding of the role of drawing in the making of architecture.

There is a distance, however slight, between a drawing as representation and what it endeavors to represent. Drawings are more than passive recipients of their authors' actions; they do more than reflect a way of seeing. They abstract vision and thought, imposing a material presence on the act of representation and thereby on imagination.[1] The conventions of drawing, the syntactical agreements for drawing constructions, like orthographic, axonometric, or perspective types, interject a discipline on the vagaries of thought. In addition, drawing tools and surfaces impose their own physical presence and influence, adding a textural aspect to the visual presence of an idea being contemplated. Each medium has tendencies which can be exploited with greater or less intensity. Pencil offers soft, subtle tones; ink the possibility of taut opaque lines; highly textured paper creates a grain; smoother paper lets a tool glide across the surface. Just as an author inserts his or her conceptual presence into a drawing through a mode of seeing, interpreting, and changing a scene, drawing tools impose a material influence. Drawing thus intervenes between an author and her or his ideas being considered, becoming in effect a third presence. In this sense, drawing is not a transparent translation of thought into form but rather a medium which influences thought just as thought influences drawing.[2]

Drawings also have their own lifetime, persisting beyond the moment of execution and initial reception and influencing those who view them. Once a drawing has been completed, its author is absent and mute. The influence of a drawing then exists independently, acquiring its own voice and its own history through many acts of viewing and interpreting. A powerful drawing may last decades, its physical presence continuing to make a vision indelible.

In the workings of most architectural offices, the authorship of specific drawings is often difficult to ascertain, as many hands may play a role in their production. For example, many of the perspectives from the office of Frank Lloyd Wright were constructed by assistants, after which Wright added shading, entourage elements, or color. When specifically known, authorship has been indicated, but in many cases it is possible that drawings attributed to an individual may have been worked on by several others.

Drawing is only one of many media used in the production of architecture, but in our opinion, it is the essential medium. Architects also employ written and spoken language, three-dimensional models, electronic media, and even other buildings as a means to designing. Computer-generated drawings are a unique contemporary means of representation, produced by a tool with intelligence that can open new areas and possibilities. These capabilities allow for the convenient visualization of complex shapes, which are sometimes extremely difficult to construct by hand. The technology of computer graphics is quickly developing and its impact, though still unfolding, will undoubtedly affect architectural representation in a very substantial way. The use of the computer for architectural drawings has already influenced the development of drawing skills and will increasingly continue to do so. However, in this book, the focus is on the effects of drawing done by hand because of its long tradition, formative aspect, and ongoing role. Despite the fact that all of the examples in this book have been drawn by hand, the issues that are raised are relevant to computer-generated drawings as well.

The book is divided into two sections after an introductory chapter analyzing in detail the use of drawing by Le Corbusier. The first section focuses on drawing types, discussing constructional methods and implications of orthographic, axonometric, and perspectival drawings. Each chapter in this section includes an explanatory note at the end for those unfamiliar with the conventions of the drawing type being discussed. The second section illustrates different applications of architectural drawings, including referential, diagrammatic, design, presentation, and visionary drawings. Each chapter of this section includes drawings of different drawing types, as the emphasis in the second section is not on formal taxonomies but rather on the differences in attitudes and purposes toward drawing. The book concludes with a tenth chapter on generalized issues of representation.

A drawing is like a theatrical scrim, a gauzelike screen whose properties change dependent on lighting conditions. Like a scrim, a drawing is both opaque and translucent, a filter between the drawer and viewer, drawer and object, between ideas conceived and their two-dimensional manifestation. A scrim and a drawing both prevent as well as allow view, asserting their presence with varying authority and in different ways. When the back light turns on, the scrim disappears. In a similar way, drawings dissolve and open a world of rich possibilities.

Chapter 1

The Lessons of Drawing for Le Corbusier

The graphic legacy of Charles-Éduoard Janneret, also known as Le Corbusier, demonstrates the importance of drawing to his design process and suggests its potential impact for all. One of the most influential of twentieth century architects, he was a quintessential drawer, using drawings to record existing phenomena, generate ideas, develop their potential, and present to others. He compulsively sketched ideas and artifacts, utilized precise drawings to test design solutions, regularly searched through his collection of sketchbooks for inspirations, and employed carefully considered finished drawings as a means to convince others of his ideas. Drawing for him was both private and shared, a means to research the past as well as to explore the new.

He fully exploited the possibilities of drawing, using various drawing types to advantage and using drawing in different manners and for a variety of purposes. The way he used drawing as a necessary mode of designing and his drawings themselves serve even today as a model and inspiration for many. Whether working in pen or pencil, freehand or hardline, drawing was the beginning point of his design explorations. It is impossible to talk about the evolution of Le Corbusier's designs without talking about the evolution of his drawings. What do these graphics say about the influence of drawing on the architecture of Le Corbusier? How did drawings relate to his working process? What might one learn about architectural drawing and design by looking at the example of Le Corbusier?

Le Corbusier maintained sketchbooks throughout his career. Although he could sketch wonderfully, they contain few masterful drawings: his drawings often violate perspectival conventions or distort proportions, and sometimes the subjects are barely recognizable.[1] His concern was not with accuracy in the sense of shape or proportion or the quality of a drawing as a finished product. Instead his writings indicate a different intent. As described in *Towards a New Architecture*, Le Corbusier believed in an order for all things. His aim was to design buildings which would give users the measure of this order—moving their emotions and attaining harmony. The important task for him was to try to discover this underlying order and through these discoveries bring his forms into line with it. Drawing played a key role in this search:

I would like architects—not just students to pick up a pencil and draw a plant, a leaf, the *spirit* of a tree, the *harmony* of a sea shell, formations of clouds, the complex play of waves spreading out on a beach, so as to discover different expressions of an *inner force*. I would like their hands and minds to become *passionately involved* in this kind of intimate investigation. (Emphasis provided.) (Guiton 1981,83)

Note that in this quote he refers not to the shape of a tree, but to its "spirit," not to the lines of a seashell but to its "harmony." His concern in other words is not so much with recording the surface appearance of an object, with a picturesque rendition of a phenomenon, but rather with drawing as a means to become "passionately involved," that is, to enter into a kind of intuitive communion with the object. For him, drawing offers the possibility to connect to some "inner force," to find some unseen quality, a presence underlying a shape. His intent is to somehow erase the barrier between the drawer and the subject of the drawing by entering fully into the act of drawing. His drawings aim to tease out an unseen essence, to go beyond the surface to find conditions of order and harmony.

For this reason, he habitually recorded impressions of the world around him as well as inspirations for his projects in small bound sketchpads (usually 4-by-7-inches, varying from 3-by-5-inches to as large as 6-by-9-inches). These sketchbooks are omnipresent, visual journals in which he draws with rapid calligraphic strokes. Their subject matter is eclectic, as he draws and thereby attempts to understand the "inner force" underlying a full range of objects and viewpoints, from bulls or landscapes, views from a jeep or an airplane, from nudes to scuppers. For example, the drawing of a cow and its calf (Figure 1.1) shows Le Corbusier's fascination with their forms and in particular with their profiles. In one of the many

Figure 1.1 Le Corbusier: Cow with calf, 1950. Sketch. Ink and pencil. (© 1992 ARS, New York/SPADEM, Paris).

drawings that he did of cows, bulls, or oxen, he repeats lines again and again along the contours of the cow, as if calculating its shape. He feels along the spine of the animal with his pen, setting the inner nuances of its shape into the recesses of his mind. In the making of this drawing he does more than record, he remakes the profile into a new format, a critical and creative two-dimensional restatement. His sketchbooks contain a number of studies of various subjects curvilinear shapes; he sketches them in order to closely examine and attempt to understand and remember better their nuances. A drawing from an airplane passing over Colombia (Figure 1.2) depicts how he metaphorically connects the sight of a meandering river joined to a network of marshes with ideas of automobiles. The notes on the

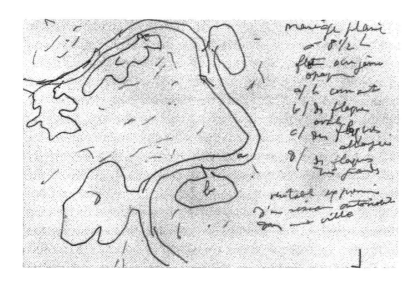

Figure 1.2 Le Corbusier: View from an airplane, 1951. Sketch. (© 1992 ARS, New York/SPADEM, Paris).

Figure 1.3 Le Corbusier: Pyramid and sphinx, Egypt, 1952. Sketch. Ink and colored pencil. (© 1992 ARS, New York/SPADEM, Paris).

page read: "swamp plain at 8:30 am opaque yellow ochre water a/ the current b/ oval pools c/elongated pools d/ very large pools *veritable expression of an automobile network in a city.*" (Emphasis provided.)

He continuously pursued this way of representing phenomena and through drawing the remaking of visual experience. By sketching existing phenomena, he tests and reiterates his ideas for space and form, such as in this memorable drawing of a pyramid and sphinx (Figure 1.3). Executed appropriately in sandy-colored pencil and black ink, he presents sphinx and pyramid in stark juxtaposition as if no distance separates them, graphically pulling them together into a tight compressed relationship by treating values the same for both elements. He emphasizes the profile of elements against the sky, studying carefully the way a built form meets the sky, and impresses the effect of their silhouettes into his memory. In a powerfully spatial drawing done on board a ship (Figure 1.4) he depicts the sense of compression created by the horizontal plane of floor and "roof" and the resultant sense of release offered by the long ribbon opening. His writings indicate his enthusiasm for the forms and symbols of planes and ships, and drawings like this are a means to study their effects and to test his own spatial conceptions by comparing them to forms in a different context.

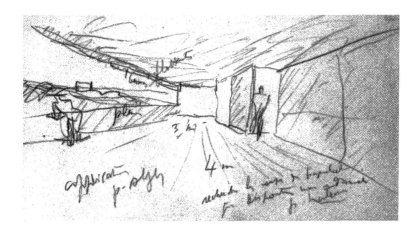

Figure 1.4 Le Corbusier: View of a ship's promenade, 1933. Sketch. Pencil. (© 1992 ARS, New York/SPADEM, Paris).

These drawings (Figures 1.1 through 1.4) are far from careful, journalistic depictions of surface form, and they show little concern for the accuracy of their depiction or their beauty as end products. Instead they are ruminations, patterns of analytical lines, a means to intensify vision and memory of a specific place by interpreting a view through drawing. The sketches were private, unself-conscious, and rarely shown to outsiders. As intimate diaries of his vision, these drawings are a kind of internal dialogue like that of a journal. They illustrate the ways in which he observes scenes and records their essentials for later use. These drawings serve as visual notes, often supplemented by verbal ones. They are both a means to implant more firmly in his memory a seen condition as well as remind him of it after the fact. The sketchbooks constitute a collection of *references*, of drawings done from observation alluding to specific scenes, which could be subsequently reobserved through the graphic and revitalized as a visual source. These **referential drawings** were a key resource which he maintained throughout his life and to which he frequently referred while working on projects.[2]

Le Corbusier often carried several past sketchbooks with him when he was working on new projects. His contemporaries have described how he kept his books in a drawer and often looked through them. The sketches in them were important sources for the development of his designs, as they provided a rich resource of forms, remembered both as visual experiences and as drawn visions.[3] For example, in a vivid description of the multiple inspirations for the Chapel of Ronchamp, Daniele Pauly refers to his diverse store of drawings from travel, personal experiences, and contemporary technology, from phenomena as diverse as a crab shell, a method of daylighting seen at the Villa Adriana at Tivoli (Figure 1.5), an airplane wing, a ski jump (Figure 1.6), a hydraulic dam, and building

Figure 1.5 Le Corbusier: Villa Adriana at Tivoli, Italy. Pencil and colored pencil on gridded sketchbook paper. (© 1992 ARS, New York/SPADEM, Paris).

forms from North Africa (Figure 1.7). She explains, "it was obviously not a question of compiling a kind of catalogue of forms or models but rather one of retaining ideas and solutions, of noticing analogies of forms attributable to analogies of function." She cites his constant practice of sketching as the key to his creative process wherein he merged multiple entities into a new synthesis (Pauly 1987, 131).

Perhaps the most revealing aspect of his sketchbooks is the lack of formal differences between his referential drawings and his **design drawings**, those graphics used to discover and develop the forms of an emerging project. Whereas referential drawings focus on preexisting phenomena, design drawings depict forms from the imagination of their makers.

His sketchbooks contain both types of drawings, and it is often difficult to decipher which are which. It is as if he made no

Figure 1.6 Le Corbusier: Chapel at Ronchamp, France. 1951. Sketches. Ink and colored pencil. (© 1992 ARS. New York/SPADEM, Paris).

Figure 1.7 Le Corbusier: A rural church, c. 1935. Sketch. Pencil. (© 1992 ARS, New York/SPADEM, Paris).

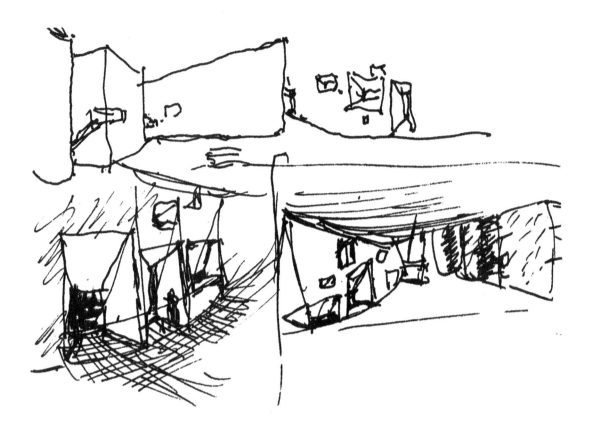

Figure 1.8 Le Corbusier: Chapel at Ronchamp, France, 1951. Interior perspectives. Ink and colored pencil. (© 1992 ARS, New York/SPADEM, Paris).

distinction in his mind between the two, just as he made no distinction in his sketchbooks between drawing an existing condition as contrasted to a thought for design. For example, a drawing for the Chapel of Ronchamp (Figure 1.8) shows the same quick, almost messy manner of indicating a form/idea as he used to record visual references of existing phenomena. These four interior perspective views illustrate his typical hurried style, rough and distorted, but they show the first drafts of his visual ideas to himself.

As Le Corbusier referred to his sketching as a means to become "passionately involved" with a condition and to find some "inner force," design was a similar but reversed procedure. Instead of entering into a kind of intuitive connection with a given object, he attempts to discover within himself the new object which would have an intuitive fit with program, site, and circumstances. In other words he seeks to tap into the multiplicity of remembered forms and images and connect them to a project at hand. He did this both consciously and unconsciously, leafing through his old sketchbooks to remind himself of past experiences as well as actively sketching as a means to

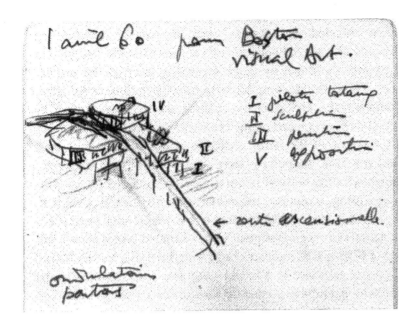

Figure 1.9 Le Corbusier: Carpenter Visual Arts Center, Harvard University, Boston, Massachusetts, 1960. Sketch. Ink and colored pencil. (© 1992 ARS, New York/SPADEM, Paris).

enter into a kind of contemplative search. He sought to transcend specific forms by seeking their "inner forces," allowing him to bring those essences into other contexts and, with new meanings, into ideas for his designs.

In the design of the Carpenter Visual Arts Center in Boston, the project essentially begins with a drawing from his sketchbook. A brief examination of the evolution of the design of this building reveals the various types and modes of drawing that he utilized.[4] The beginning drawing is an ideogram (Figure 1.9), a striking example of a use of drawing in which highly abstract configurations of marks cryptically represent the primary properties of a scheme. Done on the first of April 1960, it was the culmination of a four-month period of thinking about program, site, and project. This example of the kind of early exploratory sketches which he uses to seek the expression of basic ideas seems especially powerful and knowing in the ways that it captures the essentials of the project. The ramp cuts through the building in a forceful and dynamic way, with a series of repetitive nervous lines at the top emphasizing the intersection with the main volumes and the arrival and entry. A few lines of yellow pencil are used to reinforce his ink linework with color and reiterate the sense of the path. Green-colored pencil sets the building into a lush, verdant setting with plants growing from the many terraces. The volume shown to the left of the ramp is clearly a curvilinear shape. The one to the right is more ambiguous, although it seems to have a rounded corner. Crowning the building is a cylindrical volume. The building is shown elevated on columns, and his use of *ondulatoires* (rhythmically spaced vertical fins) are noted in the margin and in graphic shorthand by quick scrawling lines on the vertical faces. The entire drawing looks to have been done in minutes, spontaneously, capturing the scheme as a scheme, noting its essential elements, arranging its critical volumes in relationship to the theme of the ramp, indicating basic shapes or at least ideas for basic shapes of curve and cylinder, and beginning thoughts for the vertical relationships of functions (notes indicate painting, sculpture, and exhibition). So this tiny, rudimentary, almost crude drawing (drawn in a 4-by-7-inch sketchpad, the actual drawing measures 2½-by-2-inches and is shown full size in Figure 1.9) indicates beginning thoughts for his formal language, response to site and program, and, essentially, the direction that he will pursue for the duration of the project. The eventual building is predicted by the sketch, but does not match the sketch. It sets an open-ended direction for investigation.

Following this early conceptual sketch, he and his office began work on the project in earnest by undertaking a series of drawings studying the scheme in greater detail and with increasing levels of development and accuracy. These more detailed design drawings include a sequence of hardline and freehand studies, which are used to refine and elaborate the initial ideas depicted by the conceptual sketch, and are instrumental in transforming the initial idea into a finished design. An early plan study (Figure 1.10) done ten days after his conceptual sketch shows an S-shaped ramp cutting between two lunglike volumes. Done in pencil rather than the ink and colored pencil of his sketchbook drawing, the lines here seem less rushed and emphatic, more searching, more open, broken in places like a dotted line as he allows the pencil to touch and then to skip a spot, then touch back down again. The lines seem to search for the correct configuration and relationship of the key masses. As he works on these particular shapes, the relationship of his design studies to his referential studies of other curvilinear forms, such as the cow and river (Figures 1.1 and 1.2), becomes clearer. The relationship is not one of direct correspondence, where his curve looks exactly like a curve drawn before, rather it is one of intuitive transformation where he studies many existing curves in his sketchbooks in order to be able to have a deeper understanding of how his own curves should work. It is as if he put the curves he saw into himself through the sketch and then let them out again through the drawing to merge with particular project needs, finding, in effect, a new form.[5]

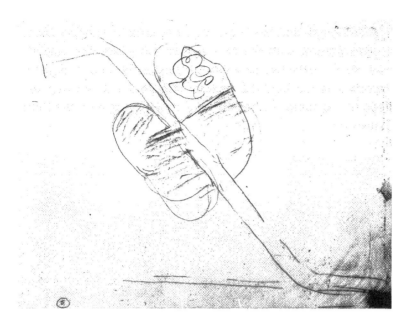

However, there is an important difference between this freehand plan study and his sketchbook drawings. For he has moved from the gestural ideogram to the kind of larger scaled study that will test and develop the idea. The drawing here is to scale and measures 18-by-24-inches. Simultaneously, a critical series of hardline drawings were being studied and prepared while Le Corbusier worked. These drawings were primarily done by his codesigner, Jullian de la Fuente, and their record points out the necessary dialectical relationship between the free hand and the hard line (or restrained hand). For example, two drawings study important aspects of the ramp at approximately the same time period as the plan drawing above. The hardline plan drawing of the ramp (Figure 1.11) shows the

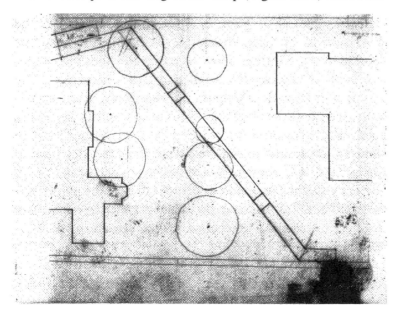

required length and landings, the fit relative to existing trees, the intersection with the two streets and sidewalks, and its relationship to the two neighboring existing buildings. Equally important is the hardline section (Figure 1.12) showing the slope of the ramp, its length, and its merging with the third floor-level.

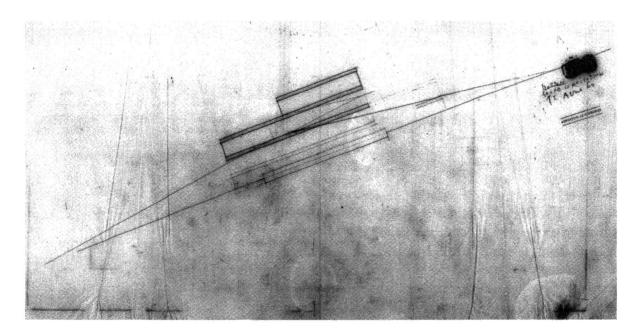

Figure 1.12 Le Corbusier: Carpenter Visual Arts Center, Harvard University, Boston, Massachusetts, 1960. Section. Pencil, colored pencil on trace, 23″ × 35⅝″. (© 1992 ARS, New York/SPADEM, Paris).

Contrast these drawings to the gestural ideogram: The ideogram shows a ramp moving up and through a building; its length, slope, exact condition of intersection with existing walks and ground as well as with the new interior spaces are unspecified. Nothing is specific except for the *idea* of ramp which is vigorously indicated: There is a powerful sense of what the experience of the ramp should be. In contrast, the hardline developmental drawings show exact length, location, slope, and point of intersection with unequivocal accuracy. The precision of these drawings ties the idea down, albeit temporarily, indicating the pragmatic limits of an idealistic beginning point. What happens if the length of the ramp is insufficient to climb to the desired third-floor level? Does the idea have to change? As Le Corbusier worked on the project, he did find it necessary to sink the first floor in order to have the ramp reach the third floor. This indicates the extent to which he was willing to adjust the solution in response to the discoveries in these drawings.

A freehand plan drawing done by Le Corbusier two days after these hardline drawings shows the impact of these precise

studies (Figure 1.13). The ramp is slightly adjusted to allow it to bend around the tree to the top of the sheet; its entire profile is more carefully drawn, obviously traced from the hardline underlay, that is, from the drawing which was laid under the subsequent piece of trace and used to guide succeeding free-hand lines. This use of tracing paper allows the architect to draw freehand but in a much more structured manner, in a way that allows the spontaneity of the hand while still providing an accurate and measured framework. An example of a freehand adjustment in this case is the way that the two ends of the ramp gently curve in the tracing. In addition, trees are more exactly located and a notch in the building is provided to accommodate one of the trees. These adjustments indicate the importance of the development of the scheme through more exact hardline studies. Following Le Corbusier's freehand study, his assistant prepared a hardline drawing recording and restudying the study. The drawing which was done freehand over a hardline underlay thus became itself an underlay. The architects confronted precise limits in the hardline developmental drawing,

Figure 1.13 Le Corbusier: Carpenter Visual Arts Center, Harvard University, Boston, Massachusetts, 1960. Plan. Pencil, colored pencil on trace, 18″ × 23¼″. (© 1992 ARS, New York/SPADEM, Paris).

facing dimensional and formal specificity which forced them to make changes such as the notch in the plan. If studied only through ideograms like the original sketch, the change in ramp profile swerving around the tree or even the necessity to have the extra length at one end may not have been realized. In a gestural drawing, ideas stay ideas, that is, relatively amorphic and generic. As drawings become more specific, ideas are played against limits, and are transformed from ideograms to specific solutions. In the sequence of drawings, the drama of this interaction unfolds. Through the process of underlay, overlay, overlay which becomes underlay, and overlaid again, an ongoing dialogue ensues between drawings. A more developed section, which is drawn freehand in ink and delineated by white and black pencil (Figure 1.14), also shows the effect of tracing a hardline underlay. In this case, the freehand lines are structured and relatively controlled. Layers of tracing paper are used to make adjustments and to try out different possibilities, and become a critical means to study the exterior ramp in relationship to an interior ramp.

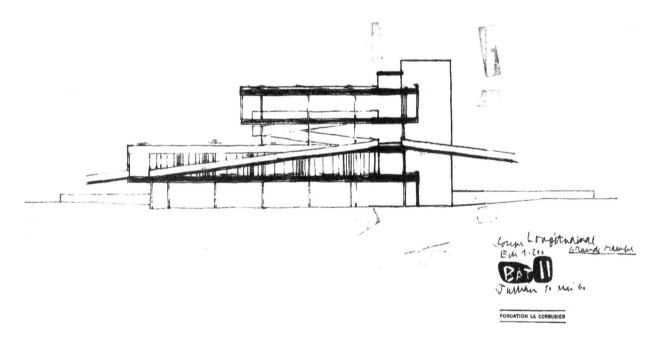

Figure 1.14 Le Corbusier: Carpenter Visual Arts Center, Harvard University, Boston, Massachusetts, 1960. Section. Pencil and colored pencil on paper with trace overlay, 17¾″ × 26″. (© 1992 ARS, New York/SPADEM, Paris).

Approximately two months after beginning their intensive period of design, after working through dozens and dozens of freehand and hardline drawings, drawings of sections, plans, and elevations, a set of drawings was prepared for presentation to the clients. This was the first exposure of the design to an outside group (that is, outside of the office). These **presentation drawings** (Figures 1.15–1.17) include a site plan, six floor

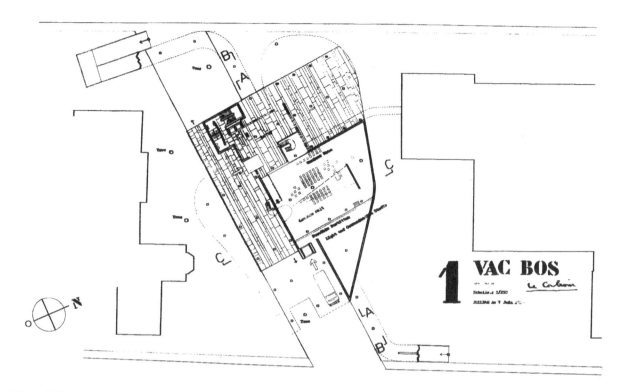

Figure 1.15 Le Corbusier: Carpenter Visual Arts Center, Harvard University, Boston, Massachusetts, 1960. Plan. India ink on tracing paper, 17¼″ × 27¼″. (© 1992 ARS, New York/SPADEM, Paris).

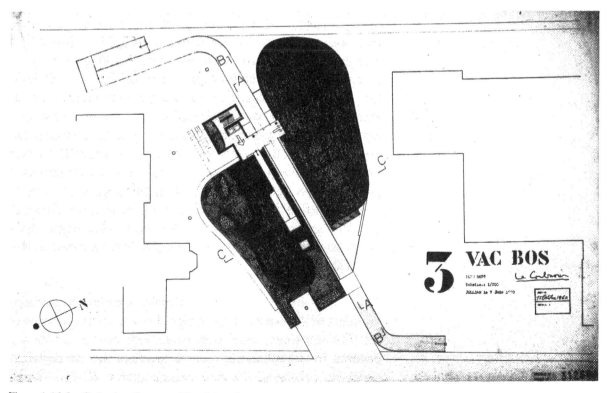

Figure 1.16 Le Corbusier: Carpenter Visual Arts Center, Harvard University, Boston, Massachusetts, 1960. Plan. Colored pencil on print, 17¼″ × 27¼″. (© 1992 ARS, New York/SPADEM, Paris).

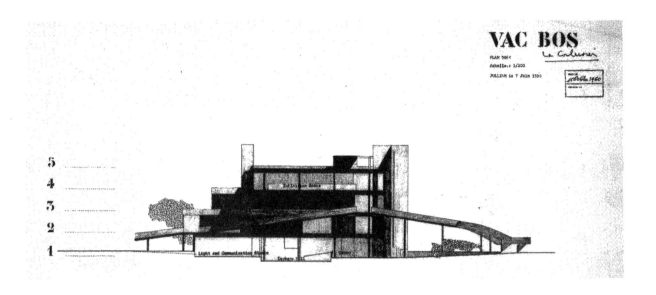

plans, and three sections. (In addition a model was presented.) The drawings are hardline ink drawings with stenciled and typed lettering, printed and delineated with color pencils in red, yellow, and gray. These precise tight drawings are replete with information, showing such details as paving patterns, furniture in various rooms, and how the exterior walls would be treated. Moreover, the treatment of the outside wall with fins and mullions is shown definitively for the first time, while precise relationships between columns and walls are established. Although previous study drawings were hardline, measured, precisely done, and show structure, outlines, stairs, and elevator, none of them had quite reached the total development of those prepared for the presentation. The act of preparing a presentation for a group of outsiders required Le Corbusier and his office to reach a higher level of detail and specificity than they had previously. A presentation represents a commitment, a point of stasis during which the working process temporarily stops, signified by the preparation of these more finished, detailed, and impressive set of drawings. This represents a symbolic threshold that states, even if only for a moment, that this is *the* design.

These drawings were self-consciously created to persuade outsiders of the merits of the design. Prior to the preparation of the final drawings, tests were made with various colors and patterns in a preliminary set, a pre-final set of drawings carefully considered for their graphic effect. Here drawings intended to convince a client were tested and consciously considered as objects, that is, as an end in themselves, to be admired for their beauty and for their persuasiveness. By comparison, for Le Corbusier and his assistants the interoffice drawings were a means to show their investigations to each other, but perhaps most importantly to show their thoughts to themselves. These were drawings that were interior to the circle working on the design. As such, they are generally rudimentary, minimal in what they show in order to study a particular issue, such as profiles of the building, the intersection of the ramp, structure, etc. They are often incomplete as drawings (a portion of a plan, for example), but they are complete for their author because they show what needs to be considered. They are cryptic, often enigmatic to an outsider studying them after the fact (for example, Figure 1.13), but for the office they focused on the issues and were unambiguously clear because they drew only what they needed to see. The study drawings aimed to reveal possibilities to one intimate with the project, whereas the delineated presentation drawings aimed to sway those not acquainted with the project.

Thus presentations aim outward for effect, whereas the drawings used in preparation of the design aim inward. However, presentation sets also have an internal effect on their makers, precisely as a result of their self-conscious drawing as object aspect. Once prepared, these finished pieces confront their makers as objects, as objective evidence of a building. Until they are made, it is much easier to consider design as a process in flux and to think of each study as a part of a flow. However, when a point of commitment must be made for a presentation and more finished materials are prepared, those materials face their viewers as "finished," that is, as points of closure and present themselves as a result, a conclusion. This is true for outsiders to the project who are usually unaware of all that has transpired in order to reach that point. What is perhaps more surprising is that even the insiders involved in the project may have their viewpoint of the design changed by their own drawings. When faced with these more complete and definitive drawings, it is easier to step outside of oneself and view the design from a more objective viewpoint. Presentation drawings remove the vagaries of freehand lines from their surfaces, presenting instead a more depersonalized representation: a world of flat tones, crisp hardlines, stenciled letters. This allows the person who made the design to view it more dispassionately and to see it in a new light. In this sense presentation drawings also turn inward, allowing architects to grasp nuances of a design from the standpoint of an "outside" viewpoint and thereby changing their internal understanding.

These drawings proved to be effective, convincing the university committee of the strength of the basic scheme. However, these "final" drawings turned out not to be final. As a result of university requests for changes in functional locations and unresolved functional and formal difficulties in the first scheme, the project changed considerably. The actual building varies considerably from that depicted in the first presentation set and reveals the dynamic, ongoing nature of architectural design. Client input, refinements in tectonic issues such as structural development, mechanical and electrical issues, and such pragmatic requirements as clearance at the freight elevator required adjustments to the design.

Figure 1.18 Le Corbusier: Carpenter Visual Arts Center, Harvard University, Boston, Massachusetts, 1960. Elevation. Pencil, colored pencil on trace, 21¼″ × 38″. (© 1992 ARS, New York/SPADEM, Paris).

What is important to note is the way that drawings were used to study and change the building after the first presentation. One example is the elevation drawing (Figure 1.18) that shows early testing of the treatment of the outside wall with a sun shading device called a *brise soleil* and his arrangement of vertical fins or *ondulatoires*. The drawing combines hardline horizontal lines, which were fixed in the design, with freehand, rather sketchily drawn indications of the fin and sunshade elements. It depicts the use of tentative freehand marks structured by a more precise hardline base as the designers test a new area of development. A second example is an interior perspective sketch by Le Corbusier (Figure 1.19), showing cylindrical columns, beams, and slab, studying intersections and spatial effects. Le Corbusier frequently used quick, cursory perspective studies like this, which he used to give himself a sense of standing in a space in order to better understand its effects. Finally, plan studies

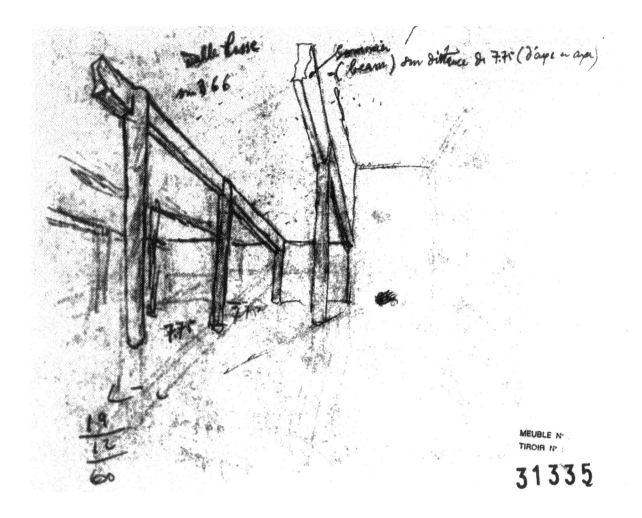

(Figure 1.20), which indicate the new direction of the second scheme, are drawn freehand, using tone to help describe the overlay of volumetric shapes and with arrows to indicate entrances and access. Note the degree of change from Figure 1.16—the two lobes now face in opposing directions and third-level functions and forms are interchanged with the second level. The drawings not only record these deliberations but also actively participate in shifting thoughts and adjusting ideas.

In concluding this brief look at the role of drawings in the design of a single building, the drawings that are preserved in the archives of the Fondation Le Corbusier indicate the diverse drawing types and manners that Le Corbusier and his employees utilized to develop this initial idea. Many of the drawings are freehand, although almost always drawn to scale. Many

Figure 1.19 Le Corbusier: Carpenter Visual Arts Center, Harvard University, Boston, Massachusetts, 1960. Perspective. 8¼″ × 10¼″. (© 1992 ARS, New York/SPADEM, Paris).

Figure 1.20 Le Corbusier: Carpenter
Visual Arts Center, Harvard University,
Boston, Massachusetts, 1961. Plans.
Pencil, colored pencil on trace, 15″ ×
39″. (© 1992 ARS, New York/SPADEM,
Paris).

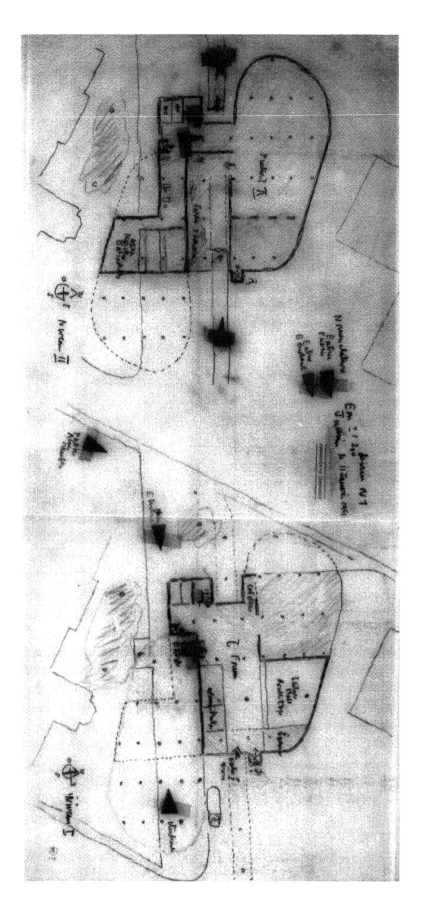

drawings are hardline, precise, and definitive. Their precision was critical in clarifying exact dimensional relationships and resolving specificities of form. Drawings vary in viewpoint, from plans to sections, elevations, and perspectives and their exact order and sense of priority vary depending on the task. For example, at one point the plan seemed to be key with elevational conditions studied after plan resolution, whereas at a different time the elevation received most of the attention and plan conditions were studied relative to the elevational ideas. The evidence of the drawings indicates several important patterns: First, the nature of the dialogue between precise hardline studies and those that are freehand; second, the absence of any set order or linear progression in the use of different drawing types, instead the sequence and focus shifts from plan to section, from elevation to plan, from plan to elevation, dependent on the moment in the project; third, the role of delineations in congealing and presenting; and finally, the importance of the design sketch that began the project—the eventual solution looks different but still seems in essence to be the same.

Drawing Types

This initial section describes the basic drawing types of architectural drawing: orthographic, axonometric, and perspective drawings. A drawing type structures a view and thereby the means of representing it. In this sense, when recording a view, perhaps the most important initial choice is deciding which drawing construct to use. Each type embodies a set of conventions that organizes the information required to make the representation. Orthographic projections, for example, depict and require measurement of two dimensions while axonometric and perspective drawings indicate three dimensions and thereby require measurements or decisions for all three. Orthographic and axonometric drawings are both *paraline* constructs where lines parallel to each other in the object remain parallel in the drawing. In contrast, the construction of perspective drawing is based on foreshortening, or a convention of drawing where parallel lines in the object are drawn as tapering toward a point and depth is indicated as "shortening" as it recedes. With these differences in mind, a drawing type becomes a viewpoint, directing one to look at the design in the way that the representation requires.

Chapter 2

Orthographic Drawings

Refer to the Explanatory Note at the end of this chapter for specific information on the conventions of orthographic drawings.

The plan has been celebrated as *the* key drawing. Le Corbusier, in *Towards A New Architecture,* refers to it as "the generator" which "holds in itself the essence of the situation":

To make a plan is to determine and fix ideas.
It is to have had ideas.
It is to so order these ideas that they become intelligible, capable of execution and communicable. It is essential therefore to exhibit a precise intention, and to have had ideas in order to be able to furnish oneself with an intention. A plan is to some extent a summary like an analytical contents table. In a form so condensed that it seems as clear as crystal and like a geometric figure, it contains an enormous quantity of ideas and the impulse of an intention (Le Corbusier 1986, 179).

His words propose that a plan is a concentration of intent, as a holder of meaning. In the lines of this drawing, Le Corbusier somehow sees the clarity of geometry and a multiplicity of ideas. As a plan reduces the three-dimensional complexity of a building to a two-dimensional simplification of its horizontal aspects, he sees not only a represented building, but ideas, intentions, and impulses that generate the shapes and underscore the project.

By reducing the amount of information, the plan emphasizes specific aspects of the building, as do its companion drawings, the section and the elevation. These orthographic drawings are relatively simple to generate in comparison to the more complex demands of axonometry or the even more intricate requirements of perspectival construction. Yet in many ways these simplest of drawings are conceptually sophisticated constructs. Each orthographic drawing eliminates information of one dimension to increase the clarity and focus on the other two: The plan represents length and width but not height; the elevation and section each represent only length and height or width and height.

The reduction of a three-dimensional construct to two dimensions is at once a hindrance and an aid to visualization. Since the third dimension is not shown, the sense of depth is compressed or flattened. On the other hand, the plan and section cut through the building, opening up its interior to view, allowing certain aspects and relationships to be seen which might not otherwise be visible. In these drawings, visual relationships are established between parts of a building by juxtaposing them in ways that might not be readily perceivable when walking through the completed building. Seeing elements such as rooms, walls, or columns drawn next to each other in a plan or section leads to conceptual connections between them, for example, comparing and contrasting their configurations, arrangements, or relative sizes. When one is in a building, one might not perceive that columns in three or four different rooms are aligned in a straight line, but a plan drawing readily indicates this. In each case the information depicted in the drawing is emphasized and enhanced by the absence of the information eliminated by the drawing's conventions. This allows the author to focus on those considerations that are depicted in the view.

Each drawing construct promotes a certain way of thinking about and quite literally looking at a design. Each isolates some aspect of the architectural design task by virtue of a particular bias posed by constructional convention and by the nature of the view produced. The plan view presents horizontal arrangements and organization, showing such aspects as the shape and configuration of the rooms' boundaries, the horizontal connections from space to space within the scheme and from inside to out, or the alignment of bearing elements. The bold **floor plans** of Ludwig Mies van der Rohe exemplify the emphasis that one architect places on this drawing type. His plans are a search for fineness, serving to refine the design in a process akin to distillation, and allowing him to slowly clarify and reach points of reductive simplicity. Mies did dozens of plan studies for his designs, many of them changed through subtle distinctions like a slightly different location for a single wall.[1] Three plan studies for the Ulrich Lange House project of 1935 demonstrate the general effectiveness of the plan drawing as well as Mies's characteristically detailed use of the drawing to study horizontal relationships. Of the large preserved body of plan drawings from the project, some are freehand sketches, some meticulously drafted and of presentation quality, but the large majority are drafted studies full of freehand marks indicating enhancement, speculation, correction, and emphasis. Each sheet reveals graphic evidence of special moments of insight, enthusiasm, diversion, redirection, emphasis, or focus.

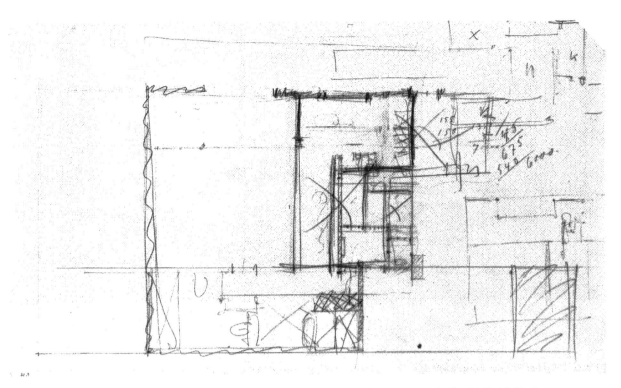

Figure 2.1 Mies van der Rohe, Ludwig: Ulrich Lange house, 1935. Plan. Pencil on tracing, 12¼″ × 21½″. (Collection, Mies van der Rohe Archive, The Museum of Modern Art, New York. Gift of the architect).

An early drawing (Figure 2.1) shows the use of the drawing to indicate initial configurations and dimensions, which then serve as a basis for changes in the development of the plan. The plan is full of alterations in architectonic elements, spatial emphasis, and drawing manner (hardline to freehand, and back again). Redrawings, overlays, and erasures abound. Precise, lightly drafted lines establish an initial dimensional framework of horizontal and vertical regulating lines, which serve as a base for his open-ended freehand revisions. For example, he adjusts the extent and configuration of the bounding wall and supersedes an initial ruled line at the far left by a more vigorously marked freehand double line moving the wall in, emphasized by an infill of wavy lines. These changes show that basic dimensions still appear to be in question or undertermined just as the organization of small service rooms seems unfixed.

Figure 2.2 uses tone to clarify functional and spatial relationships, allowing Mies to better understand the project. The combination of dark walls, toned areas, and the white void of the main living space clarifies functional and spatial relation-

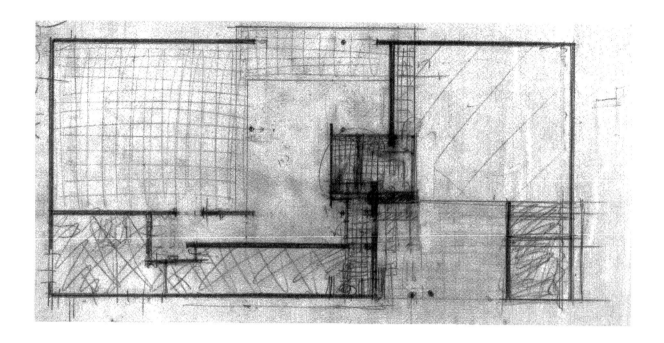

Figure 2.2 Mies van der Rohe, Ludwig: Ulrich Lange house, 1935. Plan. Pencil, colored pencil on tracing, 15¾″ × 21¼″. (Collection, Mies van der Rohe Archive, The Museum of Modern Art, New York. Gift of the architect).

ships, giving three-dimensional depth to the plan. It is based on a precisely drafted version of changes developed in previous drawings. Mies continues progressive development as he draws freehand patterns indicating major programmatic areas over the scaled and drafted base of poché walls.[2] Rapidly scrawled lines schematically indicate a gridded paving pattern in the major courtyard space to the upper left, a tile pattern in the service spaces running vertically through the middle of the scheme, and diagonal curvilinear lines highlight the bedroom areas at the bottom of the plan.

Figure 2.3 Mies van der Rohe, Ludwig: Ulrich Lange house, 1935. Plan with furniture placement. Pencil on tracing, 14½″ × 21″. (Collection, Mies van der Rohe Archive, The Museum of Modern Art, New York. Gift of the architect).

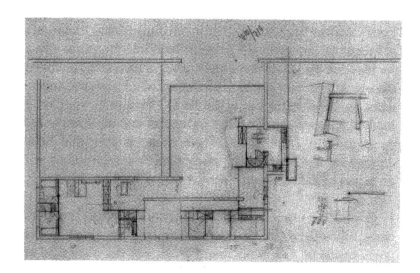

Throughout his career, Mies combined freehand, sketchier plan studies with precise, hardline drafted drawings in order to bring his designs to a high degree of refinement. This is illustrated by Figure 2.3, where Mies organizes and carefully orders the major elements of the scheme: Walls, partitions, interior and exterior spaces, transparent planes and windows, and material changes in the ground plane are all positioned and drawn with precision. Even some furniture is drawn in the sleeping areas. Committing to specific dimensional and proportional relationships in the precisely drafted base, Mies fixes the design. Yet freehand marks indicate that some ideas and details are being reconsidered. He tests furniture locations in the master bedroom, considers closet lengths, door swings, and a few partition positions in the small bedroom area. On the right side of the drawing, Mies draws perspective sketches to test the plan conditions in three dimensions. Though these freehand marks indicate refinements no longer requiring wholesale adjustments, they nonetheless show Mies's preoccupation with the ongoing process of distillation, clarifying and purifying the scheme down to its smallest scale.

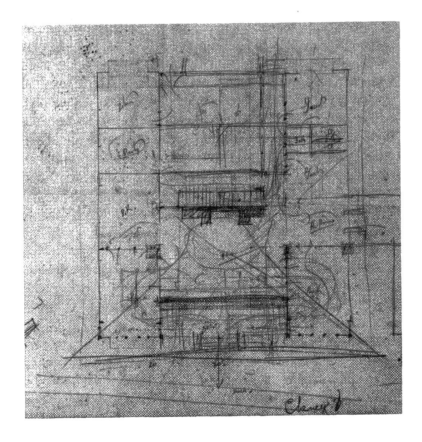

Figure 2.4 Frank Lloyd Wright: Cheney House, Oak Park, Illinois, 1903. Sketch plan. (Courtesy of The Frank Lloyd Wright Archives. Copyright © The Frank Lloyd Wright Foundation 1985).

A plan represents the formal order of columns, walls, openings, and floor surface patterns, a depiction of the physical features of the building. It can also diagram space and movement, and trace the paths of future occupants. In Frank Lloyd Wright's scratchy sketch of the Cheney House in Oak Park, Illinois (Figure 2.4), this path is literally traced by a pencil, allowing Wright to visualize the movement of an imaginary inhabitant. The track of his pencil climbs the stairs to enter, moves through a connecting hallway, crosses thresholds into rooms, and eddies around in them for awhile. The mark retraces paths, moving back and forth, from room to room, from inside to the outside terrace and back, circling through connecting rooms and within a room. Other path-marks trace the procession from reception room and circle the area in front of the hearth, the symbolic and ceremonial center to Wright's residential architecture. Similar marks also confirm the paths of functional convenience, as for example the semicircular stroke that designates the route from the guest room in the upper right corner to the adjacent bath. It is as though Wright is exploring the building by placing himself into the scheme through the drawing.

A **site plan** depicts a building's relationship to its setting. In his sketch of the master plan of the National Capitol, Dacca, Bangladesh (Figure 2.5), Louis Kahn uses rich, dark charcoal strokes to give the new government center a vivid presence on the sheet, allowing him to visualize the three-dimensional impact on the site. In the left half of the drawing he renders the ground in closely hatched black marks while leaving the buildings untoned. Thus the white buildings project from the dark background in a powerful sense of three-dimensional relief. The drawing depicts an aerial view of the complex, transcending diagrammatic abstraction by adding detail and definition and placing the viewer in position over the project. The plan also shows the major buildings aligned by a conceptual axis which signifies their symbolic importance in the governmental complex, fixes their relationship in the drawing and anticipates the experience one will have in the constructed project.

In a site plan for the City Hall and Central Library of The Hague in the Netherlands (Figure 2.6), Richard Meier and Partners show the project in relationship to the surrounding urban condition, tying the new to the existing fabric. The building is drawn to the same scale and in the same way as every other structure, except for the amount of detail: The new building is

distinguished by its articulated roofscape while the surrounding buildings are shown with much less detail. Both the new City Hall and the adjacent buildings, however, are given height by *cast shadows*, a simple and conventional device to enhance three-dimensionality, where relative lengths of shadows correspond to measured depths according to a precise constructional process. This technique allows the indication of three-dimensional information in orthographic projections which reveal only two. Meier's drawing of meticulously precise, mechanically ruled black lines and solid black tones conveys striking depth for a drawing of such severely constrained vocabulary.

As the plan cuts horizontally through a building, a **section** cuts through it vertically. In his 1990 renovation project of the Reichstag Building (Figure 2.7), Gottfried Böhm uses the section to bring out vertical relationships of space, to depict the verticality or horizontality of the surrounding building, and to show the spaces between it and the new assembly hall. The drawing cuts through the existing courtyard building, floating the new construction in the middle. His masterful graphic technique contrasts the old, drawn lightly and freehand, with the new, represented by more heavily toned and ruled lines.

Figure 2.5 Louis I. Kahn: National Capitol, Dacca, Bangladesh, 1973. Master plan. Pencil and red pencil on trace, 12″ × 16″. (Copyright 1977 Louis I. Kahn Collection, University of Pennsylvania and Pennsylvania Historical and Museum Commission).

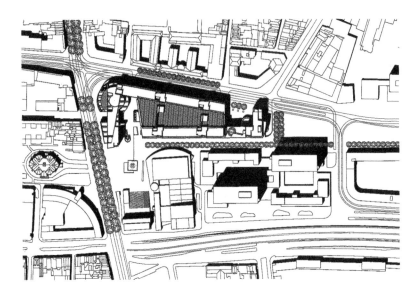

Figure 2.6 Richard Meier & Partners, Architects: The Hague City Hall and Central Library, The Hague, 1986–1994. Site plan.

Graphite toning brings out the qualities of enclosure, structure, and light, and reveals the project as an airy assemblage of filtered sunlight, where delicate shadows are cast through the skylit assembly area, expressing the volume and atmosphere of the structure.

In a study for the Great Hall at Principia College (Figure 2.8), Bernard Maybeck uses the section to test alternative roof shapes and possible effects of natural light. The drawing indicates the struggle to visualize, draw, and shape a project. He utilizes the graphic to imagine, draw, and imagine anew in response to the vision shown through the drawing. His pastel technique creates a rich overlay of tonal areas as he draws, erases, and draws again over his previous marks. He emphasizes certain roof and wall profiles with black chalk, clarifying and solidifying specific shapes from the tonal background.

In one of the thinnest and longest drawings in this book, Louis Kahn cuts a section through the middle of his Kimbell Museum in Forth Worth, Texas (Figure 2.9), and through the surrounding site. The use of a **site section** that extends well beyond the boundaries of the building reinforces the conception of the building as joined to the space of its setting. The park to the left is shown gradually sloping down toward a set of steps, the fountain, and eventually to the entry space of the museum. The drawing also clearly delineates the lower parking entry level and the handling of the height change in the site. Finally and perhaps most importantly, the drawing represents the low horizontal sense of the building fitting into a long horizontal band of trees, showing its nonassuming mass and gentle relationship to its site.

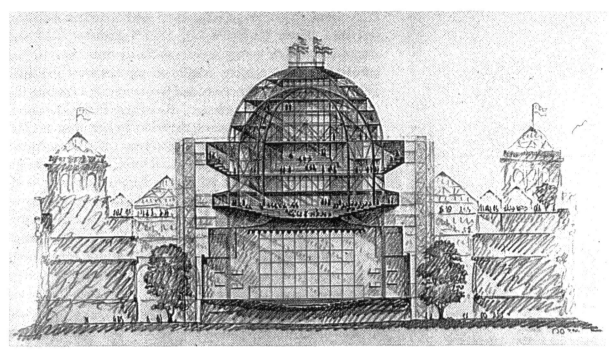

Figure 2.7 Gottfried Böhm: Reichstagsgebäude, Berlin, 1990. Section. Pencil.

Figure 2.8 Bernard Maybeck: Project for the Great Hall, Principia College, Elsah, Illinois, c. 1934. Section. Pastel on trace. (Property of Principia College).

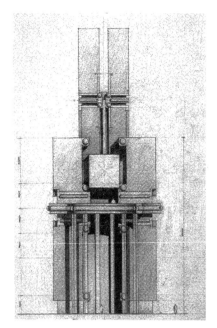

Figure 2.10 Shin Takamatsu: Kirin Plaza, Osaka, Japan, 1987. Elevation.

In an **elevation** studying the facade of the Kirin Plaza Building in Osaka, Japan (Figure 2.10), Shin Takamatsu uses cast shadows and subtle toning in order to clarify three-dimensional information. The relative length of the shadows indicates explicitly the depth of recesses and projections and clarifies the third (and previously unindicated dimension) in this elevation: the colonnaded entry advances; the white square projects. The shading also causes the tower at the top to recede. The increased precision necessary to study detail and refinements as a design progresses is carried out through a hardline drawing with freehand graphite tone added. Here Takamatsu tests profiles of banding elements, the locations of curious spherical adorn-ments, and the profiles and proportions of the overscaled entry. Depth can be further reinforced by such techniques as variations in line weight, tone, or color to suggest three-dimensionality. Here, crisp lines delineate the edges, dimensions indicate heights, and the toning imparts a sense of light, texture, and materiality. The overriding effect of the drawing is a highly articulated layering of exterior surfaces and the entry colonade.

In order to understand the three-dimensional condition of a design from orthographic drawings, one must view several related orthographic projections and mentally construct a three-dimensional model. Accordingly, the projections of plan, section, and elevation are often studied and presented together, that is, as **combined views**. In the meticulous pencil delineation of a part of Cesar Pelli's Long Gallery House project (Figure 2.11), drawn by Bradford Fiske, the four views become a singularity, a visually integrated illustration of different projec-tions that transcends flatness and confirms the three-dimen-sional conditions of the building's fabric. The carefully calcu-lated relationship of the four views binds each drawing to the others as though hinged at their borders. Different views hold common projectional alignments as they stack and line up: The wall section is over the plan of the wall, aligning the height of the wall in the section with that in the elevation, and projecting the width of the skylight panes in the roof plan into alignment with the elements of the elevation. The elevation shows the

Figure 2.9 Louis Kahn: Kimbell Art Museum, Dallas, Texas, 1966. Site section. 29⅝″ × 181⅜″. (Copyright 1977 Louis I. Kahn Collection, University of Pennsylvania and Pennsylvania Historical and Museum Commission.)

composition of the facade, its assemblage, its patterns of fenestration and joinery, and its proportions (for example, the similar size and shape of the windows and the precast blocks). The section shows the hollow interior of the lintel and gutter and the construction of the foundation and floor slab; the plan shows the hollowness of the walls, the pattern of flooring, and the proportional pattern which controls the dimension of the floor paving and wall element. The roof plan shows the top of the wall and the trench of the gutter. In addition, Fiske meticu-

Figure 2.11 Cesar Pelli & Associates (draftsman, Bradford Fiske): The Long Gallery House. Plan, section, elevation. 36″ × 24″.

lously and consistently renders the textural properties of materials, precast concrete, metal mullions, and glass, even depicting the reflective and refractive properties of glass.

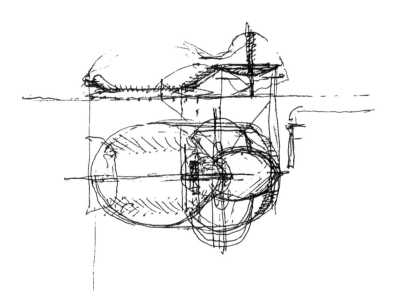

Figure 2.12 Fumihiko Maki: Fujisawa Municipal Gymnasium, Fujisawa, Japan, 1984. Plan, section.

In a series of design sketches from his book *Fragmentary Figures*, Fumihiko Maki illustrates this synergetic property of interrelated orthographic drawings where the conceptual result is greater than the sum of its parts. He is able to represent the three-dimensional qualities of his designs by combining plan views with elevations and sections. An early sketch for his design for the Fujisawa Gymnasium (Figure 2.12) shows a section drawing above the plan, connected by taut, thin projection lines which align and bind the two views, allowing a three-dimensional presence to form in the viewer's mind. Maki said of the early moments of the design: "The image I had was of a space that expanded like a bubble and while maintaining its equilibrium formed a membrane like outer skin." In spare, deft strokes, the section shows the bubblelike nature of that space in a way the plan does not convey, yet the section does not give any indication of the corresponding footprint. Thus the two drawings convey very different aspects of the emerging scheme, while the composite relationship makes certain that decisions depicted in one drawing are viewed in the other. The cross-hatching of the seats in the plan defines the shape of the gymnasium floor in width and length, while in the section the tiers of end seating help to define the shape of the space in height and length. The platform with the curved bottom in the section is revealed to be ovoid in the plan. Though actually drawn in two dimensions, each of these conditions becomes

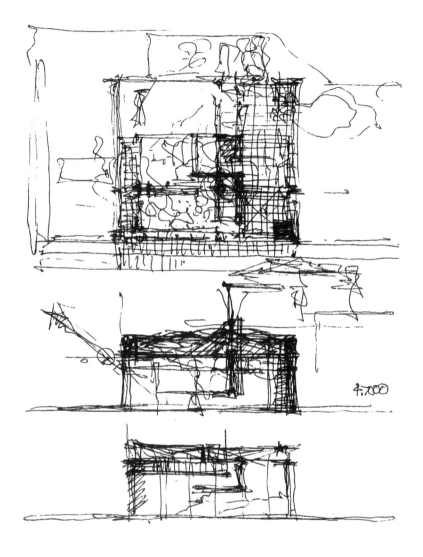

Figure 2.13 Fumihiko Maki: Tepia
Science Pavilion, Tokyo, 1989. Plan,
sections.

three-dimensional in the viewer's mind by the visual cross-
reference built into the illustration.

For the Tepia Science Pavilion in Tokyo (Figure 2.13), Maki
draws plan, elevation, and sectional views on a single sheet,
cross-referencing them by vertical alignment. In each wiry
sketch, he studies different aspects of the design without having
to immediately confront their full three-dimensional implications. As he works in plan, with height and verticality eliminated from the drawing, he is able to focus on horizontal
composition and relationships. He studies the entry sequence
and defines the circulation as an L-shaped configuration wrap-
ping around major programmatic spaces with a stair and
elevator core at the joint. Yet the adjacent section and elevation
provide constant reference and notation of the vertical condi-

tion. The vertical views depict heights, proportions, shapes, and connections. The vertical core is shown as a rising tower, hovering above the ground on an elevated base. The elevation also demonstrates his initial ideas for fenestration and entrance. Maki uses each drawing to reveal different aspects of the design while also linking the views on the sheet. Three-dimensionality is latent but present in the construct.

In a later, more developed pair of drawings which focus on the entry area of Tepia (Figure 2.14), the formal characteristics of the building's design emerge. The top drawing, which appears to be a combination of elevation and section, is shifted one bay to the left and overlaps with the plan. The drawings appear to float within each other, a kind of transparency and merging in the drawing that is reflected in the layered fabric of the building.

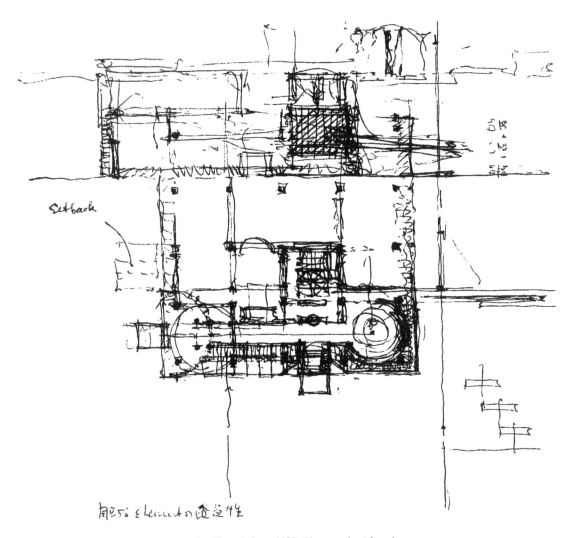

Figure 2.14 Fumihiko Maki: Tepia Science Pavilion, Tokyo, 1989. Plan, section/elevation.

In Figure 2.15 of the Maison Carré in Bazoches, France, drawings on six sheets of overlapped tracing paper illustrate Alvar Aalto's use of different orthographic drawings to study a design as well as his use of freeflowing, densely compacted sketches. As a means to enter into a mode of spontaneous discovery, he draws with a large soft pencil loosely held to produce a deliberately shaky and modulated line.[3] Sometimes barely touching the paper, he leaves faint lines and gentle, blurred impressions, marking again and again in a contemplative, searching way. Adjusting, reiterating, he tests walls, limits, spatial boundaries. The drawing concentrates his attention, allowing him to study a sequence of movement and space. His technique indicates critical areas, drawing lines repetitively, stacking strokes one on top of another, and building up values through reiteration. His drawings create a strong illusion of depth, as tone and dark edges pull walls away from the paper and simultaneously indicate key spaces.[4]

Aalto used the plan to focus his design studies, testing horizontal relationships between land and building and between one room and another. However, as shown by this sheet, he also used section and elevation sketches to view vertical conditions.

Figure 2.15 Alvar Aalto: Maison Carré, Bazoches, France, 1956–59. Plans, sections, elevations. Pencil on trace.

In a series of section studies, crisp dark lines indicate the ceiling profile of the entry space. This and several elevation drawings depict the relationship between horizontal and vertical conditions, as well as the relationship between the interior spatial profile and its exterior facade. Together these series of drawings weave a comprehensive three-dimensional representation. He habitually used plan drawings as key objects of contemplation and intuitive investigation, utilizing this type of drawing and the graphic medium of pencil to concentrate and reveal his concerns. In a second drawing showing a later, more refined plan version (Figure 2.16), Aalto sketches more specific wall locations and places furniture, doorways, and steps. Some areas appear to have been traced from earlier versions and have been drawn with a single line, while on the left side, walls and features have been drawn with repetitive lines, as if Aalto was more tentative about that part. He uses arrows to show paths of movement from car to entry hall, from lower level to upper, and from entry hall to service areas, as if he were carefully considering the experience of entry.

Orthographic drawings are forms of representation that confront their viewers with edited ways of seeing. It is their specific viewpoints and ways of looking that can alter the conceptions that authors have toward projects. Viewing a cut building from above offers the heightened possibility of seeing horizontal relationships, of seeing a collection of rooms as a whole with particular characteristics. Viewing into the interior of a building cut vertically increases the chance of seeing vertical spatial relationships, of linking previously unconnected spaces. Both present the increased possibility of visualizing order and continuity. Conceptions can be altered through the viewing of a drawing just as a drawing is changed to help to make the drawn form align more closely with a formal conception. In the formation of these conceptions, orthographic drawings play a central and generative role.

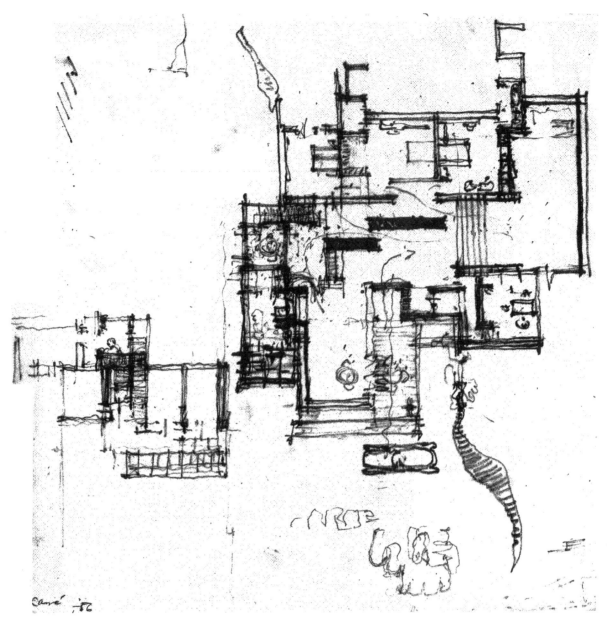

Figure 2.16 Alvar Aalto: Maison Carré, Bazoches, France, 1956–59. Plan. Pencil on trace.

Explanatory Note: Orthographic Drawing

Orthographic = ortho + graphic or straight writing. Orthographic drawings use two axes of measurement, fixed at right angles to each other. In plan, the axes measure length and width, while in section and elevation the axes measure width and height. Only two dimensions are accurately measured in each drawing; there is no provision for the direct depiction of a third dimension in the construct. In orthographic drawings, projection lines are parallel and orthogonal to the picture plane. By convention, they are also parallel to the major surfaces of the depicted project. There is no diminishment in size relative to distance along any axis and every surface of the project parallel to the picture plane is represented without distortion of shape, size, or proportion.

Each orthographic drawing cuts through the building or its site. As "flat" views without direct means of representing depth, they are either parallel to the ground (plan) or perpendicular to it (section and elevation). The cut plane of the plan is horizontal and reveals the internal arrangement of spaces as laid out per floor (Figure 2.B1). The convention presumes that the cut is made several feet above the floor (usually four or five feet, or roughly eye-level) in order to show window openings, furniture, counters and low partitions, and substantial portions of stair runs. The horizontal surfaces, especially the floor surfaces, are often elaborated in detail, as though the drawing were a kind of horizontal elevation of those interior surfaces.

The plan is a very difficult depiction to visualize because it is based on an aerial viewpoint, one which is seldom actually experienced. It is a very abstract conception, one which is perhaps more commonly encountered as mapping. When one is familiar with the use of road maps, one understands location and direction and visualizes relationships to other places on the map. It is easy to transfer that reading ability to other kinds of maps, whether of a building, shopping mall, or city area, again developing a visual sense of the place and its surrounding domain. Through this kind of practice, one develops an ability to place oneself in a map (or plan) and it makes it easier to think of a plan as a map of experience, as being in a particular place at a particular time.

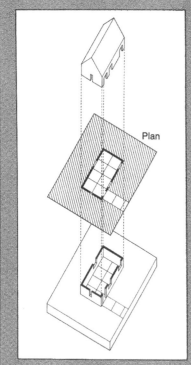

Plan

Figure 2.B1

The section cut slices vertically from top to bottom through the building and into the ground, profiling the conditions of support, span, and enclosure (Figure 2.B2). The section reveals the interior array of space in both vertical and horizontal relationship as though the exterior wall or an even more substantial portion of the building had been removed. The section cut is placed to depict the most important spatial and connective issues, such as multilevel space, skylighting, or special conditions of vertical circulation. Again, the interior surfaces are often elaborated and detailed as though the exposed walls of each revealed space was an elevation.

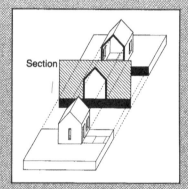

Figure 2.B2

The elevation is conceptually an exterior section, where the vertical cut is made in front of the building and cuts into the ground (Figure 2.B3). Otherwise, its conventions are virtually the same as the section.

Orthographic drawings are literally generators in that they are used to generate other drawing types such as axonometrics and perspectives which are constructed from orthographic bases plus additional third-dimensional data (as in 'plan obliques' or 'plan projection method' perspectives). Furthermore, one orthographic drawing can be the basis for another, such as a plan from which a section is projected, sharing common scale and dimensions.

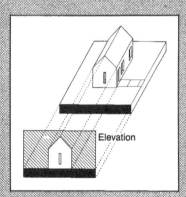

Figure 2.B3

Chapter 3

Axonometric Drawings

Refer to the Explanatory Note at the end of this chapter for specific information on the conventions of axonometric drawings.

In a stage set for Puccini's opera *Turandot*, David Hockney designed a mock Chinese painting of a pagoda set in a lake, framed by other paintings showing chairs set in a room (Figure 3.1). Done without the use of traditional linear perspective, the lines of the pagoda and chairs stay parallel in the painting. However with a change of light, the lake painting is transformed from opaque representation to translucent scrim, revealing a space beyond. Here in one moment is revealed the dilemma of representing architecture, the question of whether to retain in a drawing the qualities of the object being drawn or whether to represent instead the perceptions of a viewer, that is, whether to draw parallel lines in space as parallel or to draw them as converging. Through his set, Hockney shows the ambiguous nature of representations and the movement one experiences in looking at and representing things.

Figure 3.1 David Hockney and Ian Falconer: "Turandot" stage set, Lyric Opera of Chicago, 1992. Photograph. (Photograph by Dan Rest/ Lyric Opera of Chicago).

In the ancient tradition that Hockney recalled, commonly referred to as Chinese perspective, a convention of representation almost identical to the contemporary techniques of axonometry was used to represent depth. Lines parallel in the object being drawn were drawn parallel, rather than converging in the manner of Western perspective, and the implied viewpoint was above the scene. The desire was to utilize an artistic mode of three-dimensional representation which would produce a drawing retaining physical properties of the object being drawn, accurately representing its dimensional proportions, while at the same time giving the two-dimensional image a vivid sense of depth. In a similar manner, contemporary axonometric views retain the parallelism and scaled dimensions of the objects being drawn. Most importantly, **axonometric drawings** show three dimensions simultaneously, whereas orthographic drawings of plan, section, and elevation each describes two dimensions. An orthographic drawing can describe horizontal relationships (the plan) *or* vertical relationships (elevation and section), but none shows horizontal *and* vertical conditions. Orthogonal projections of plans, sections, or elevations reveal three dimensions in combination, but their constructions require a viewer to meld two or more drawings together in the mind in order to grasp completely the three-dimensional complexities. However, the axonometric depicts length and width in relationship to height in a single drawing while retaining the constructional convenience of paraline drawings.[1]

In a series of drawings resembling those ancient paintings in Chinese perspective, Lauretta Vinciarelli depicts the proces-

Figure 3.2 Lauretta Vinciarelli: Marfa II, Project, Marfa, 1978. Elevation oblique axonometrics. Colored pencil on mylar, 22″ × 45″.

sion and spaces of a house project in Texas (Figure 3.2) through the "objective" qualities of axonometry, consistent dimensional scale and parallelism. The **elevation oblique drawing** on the far right reveals simultaneously the space and shapes of the exterior porch in relationship to the interior spaces lying immediately behind the entry wall. The orientation looking down from above clearly shows the paths by which one can move from the porch through the main doorway into the vestibule and up the main flight of stairs. In the graphic second from the right, drawn at exactly the same scale and orientation, one arrives at the top in a large chamber with a broad flight of stairs leading to another portal. In the same view, the complete assembly of the porch is shown, depicting the front of the building in its finished form while revealing its relationship to the primary interior facade at the top of the stairs. In the two drawings on the left of Figure 3.2, Vinciarelli shows the main structure of the house in a similar way, with the first floor shown second from the left and the upper level at the far left. The drawing locates the separate parts relative to each other and to the portico, while also indicating the relationship of spaces to entry, stairs, and exterior space.

In the office of James Stirling, Michael Wilford and Associates, axonometric drawing is the locus of architectural investigation. "Axonometrics expose the spatial and volumetric composition of a design . . . [presenting] an accurate understanding of the building" through consistent parallelism and absolute measurement (Stirling 1991). Three-dimensional models are rarely used in the office's internal design procedures, and are fabricated primarily for presentation. Instead, axonometric drawings are used as the key means to study the three-dimensionality of their designs. The office's use of axonometry is comprehensive, including views up or down of the entirety of a project, more detailed views of parts of a design such as a canopy or corner, drawings which have cut away portions of a design in order to concentrate on specific areas, and graphics which focus on plan, elevation, or sectional relationships. In short, they use axonometrics to study part or whole, roof or ceiling, space or form, plan or facade.

An early example, that of the Engineering Laboratories at Leicester, England (Figure 3.3), shows a **plan oblique** view of the project that gives one a clear sense of its complex three-dimensional articulation and massing: two towers joined by vertical circulation shafts, angular auditoria jutting from the base, a split-level low horizontal mass, a tall octagonal chim-

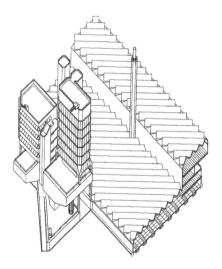

Figure 3.3 James Stirling: Engineering Building, Leicester, England, 1959. Plan oblique.

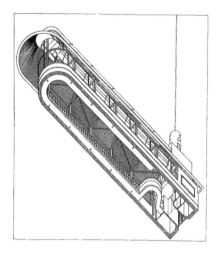

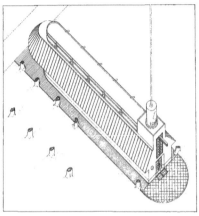

Figure 3.4 James Stirling: Electra Bookstore, Venice. Plan oblique up view and down view.

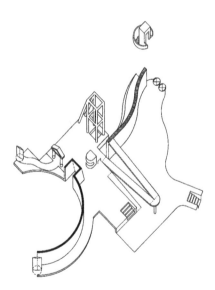

Figure 3.5 James Stirling: Museum for Northrhine Westphalia, Düsseldorf, 1975. Cut-away plan oblique.

ney, and a triangular ramp. In a single graphic, horizontal planes of roofs, terraces, ramp, and ground are shown in relation to the vertical planes of walls, planes of glass, and columns. One has a strong sense of looking down, seeing tops related to sides, providing a vivid impression of overall massing and arrangement of shapes. To understand the three-dimensional complexity of Leicester using a sequence of orthographic drawings, one would need to look at the plan and elevation, remember the heights of the masses shown in elevation, and then juxtapose them *mentally* with their plan depth and width. Instead, the axonometric juxtaposes these vertical and horizontal conditions *in the drawing*.

It is this graphic simultaneity that makes the axonometric construct such a valuable tool for three-dimensional visualization. As in the Leicester example, this drawing type allows the observer to "turn the corner" of a mass, to study the height of a tower relative to a low horizontal base, in other words to see the x, y, and z planes at the same time. The axonometric drawing also allows the designer to represent an object relative to another object, relative to the space surrounding it, and even to the space contained within a building. Within the framework of the axonometric, the designer can easily slice open the building with a horizontal (plan) and vertical (section) cuts, as shown in the lower right portion of the Leicester drawing where the interior of the lab is depicted through a sectional cut.

In two drawings by Stirling's studio of the Electra Bookstore in Venice, Italy, the relative effects of the **down view** can be contrasted to the **up view** of the Choisy or worm's-eye view.[2] The plan oblique looking down (Figure 3.4 bottom) shows roof surfaces in relationship to walls, a clerestory window, and truncated trees. The plan oblique looking up reveals the nature of interior space, switching the gaze from exterior to interior, from building as object to building as interior space. One sees ceiling, exposed structure, and a view of bookshelves from below. The building is literally detached from its ground plane, presenting a view of an object floating in air. The view hints at an environmental experience of space—looking up at things, or to be more exact, of being in a space and looking up into it. Stirling uses up and down views to dramatically alter his and others' contemplation of this specific area of the project, completely shifting the orientation and necessarily affecting one's understanding of the project.

In the drawings of Stirling's competition entry for the Museum for Northrhine Westphalia (Figure 3.5), the technique of cutting away, a form of graphic editing, focuses attention on a particular aspect or set of relationships within the design. Here, the building's envelope and many interior elements are omitted in order to reduce the amount of information and thereby emphasize the forms and spaces related to the public entry sequence. The plan oblique drawing shows the main entry doors that lead to a path along a tall, thick vertical wall and a view of a ramp that leads to a mid level and then farther up to a third level. This drawing allows one to grasp the horizontal relationships of door, wall, ramp, stair, and cylinder simultaneously with the vertical relationships of the raised floor of the mid level, the climb of the ramp, and the presence of the cylinder. Most importantly, Stirling eliminates information about other aspects of the design which might complicate the consideration of the entry sequence. The attention shifts from the walls and rooms containing the space to a consideration of the entry area as a kind of multileveled landscape articulated by objects such as the wall, ramp, cylinder, elevator, and stairs. This act of isolation, utilizing the capabilities of the axonometric representation, changes the understanding of the lobby area as shown through plan and section drawings and allows the reconsideration of the design through a radically different viewpoint.[3]

One other significant use of axonometry in Stirling's portfolio is as a format for preliminary study drawings. In the early sketches for the Fogg Museum addition (Figure 3.6), Stirling uses axonometric drawings at an early exploratory stage to sort out the relationships of the elements, investigate problems of turning the corner and of meeting the street, and to propose some initial ideas for entry. Crowded together on a sheet of tracing paper, multiple views of the emerging scheme are packed so tightly that some of the drawings overlap, sometimes even superimpose each other. Though the roster of drawing types on the sheet includes site plans, floor plans, sections, and what apear to be elevations, almost one half of the drawings are axonometric, either plan or elevation obliques. Some of these drawings are diagrammatic, showing form as an aggregation of cubes and cylinders, other sketches represent more accurately the mass and configuration of a building, but the orientation of views is held consistent throughout the sheet. With a fixed orientation, Stirling moves from one graphic inquiry to the next, each endeavor building on the previous one in a sequence of evolutionary experiments. The sketches seem to be the products of free and almost impulsive movements made in the pursuit of a specific query or inspiration.

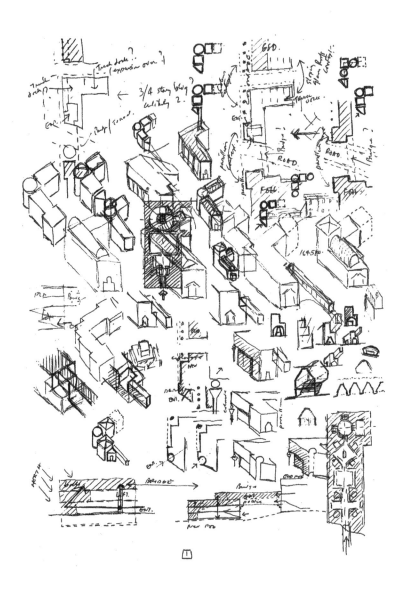

Figure 3.6 James Stirling: Fogg Museum
New Building, Cambridge, Massachusetts,
1979. Plan obliques, plans, sections.
Colored pencil on trace.

Ulrike Wilke uses a plan oblique up view (Figure 3.7) to depict
the main interior spaces of her entry in the Museum of Scotland
competition, carried out in consultation with Stirling, Wilford
and Associates. The result is a vivid sense of spatial three-
dimensionality wherein the continuum of spaces is shown
connecting the new addition's entry and arrival space to the
refurbished exhibit space embedded within the massive old
building. The drawing indicates the sequence of places that
visitors will experience as they move through the museum. The
viewer is located below ground looking up into the interior at
the walls and ceilings and other elements that are the most
prominent definers of the primary space's character, size, and
shape. The stipple pattern which tones the ceiling strongly
defines that plane, providing a clear background from which the
walls, columns, and display elements project, and visually
emphasizes the volume of the revealed spaces.

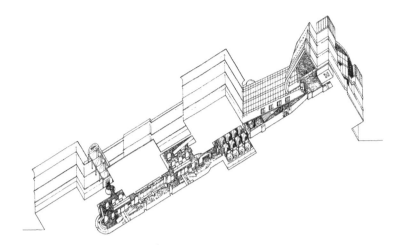

Figure 3.7 Ulrike Wilke, M.Arch. (in consultation with Stirling, Wilford and Associates): Museum of Scotland project, Edinburgh. Plan oblique up view.

In the construction of axonometric drawings, the orientation of architectural elements relative to the horizontal and vertical edges of the sheet make a dramatic difference in the resultant look and graphic clarity of the drawing. For example, Wilke turns one set of planes at a thirty degree angle and the second at a sixty degree angle relative to the horizontal. As a result, the long side of the building is shown "flatter," with greater clarity and emphasis. Length, width, and height each have their own direction in her drawing. However, in a second example of an axonometric up view, William Bricken orients one set of planes

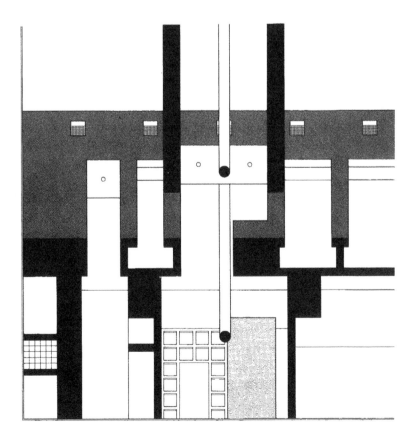

Figure 3.8 William Bricken: Architectural office, St. Louis. Plan oblique up view. Ink on mylar. (Property of Fred Powers and Associates)

parallel to the horizontal axis and the second parallel to the vertical one (Figure 3.8). His format reduces the axes of three dimensions (width, length, and height) to a matrix of vertical and horizontal lines, producing an abstraction of striking simplicity. However, a certain graphic ambiguity results as the vertical edges of wall openings are aligned with the horizontal conditions of one set of walls. Bricken uses tone to clarify the drawing with the darkest value indicating the cut conditions at the base of walls or columns, medium greys indicating the faces of vertical planes, and finally, white coding ceilings and other horizontal surfaces.

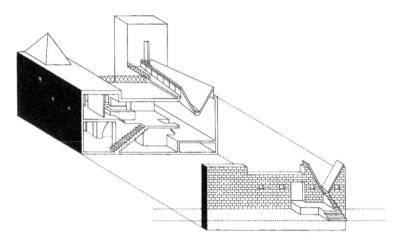

Figure 3.9 Steven Holl: Metz House, Staten Island, 1980. Cutaway elevation oblique.

Steven Holl uses axonometric drawings to represent specific concepts of his projects. For example, in the drawings for the Metz house (Figure 3.9), he uses an elevation oblique to show the facade delaminated and moved forward from the rest of the house. The opaque and masklike quality of the facade obscures the character of the space behind it, but by pulling it away, the drawing reveals the freely configured, flowing spaces of the interior and the skylight. At the same time it maintains a sense of the facade's effect on the character of the interior spaces, by showing the size and placement of the apertures. Thus the graphic delamination makes it easy to see otherwise invisible relationships.

Another example of Holl's advantageous use of the convenience and coordinate structure of the axonometric format is found in this drawing of the Berkowitz House in Martha's Vineyard (Figure 3.10). Here he uses an **exploded view** to show the major parts and components, producing the effect of a

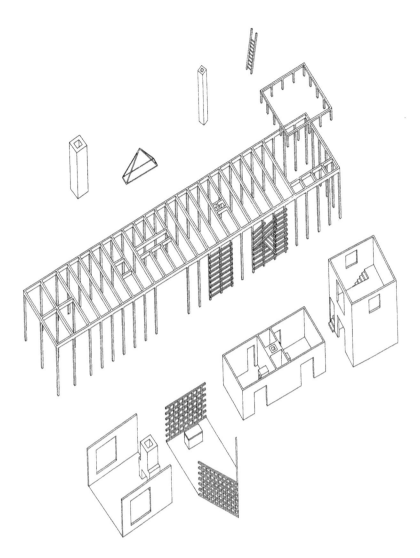

Figure 3.10 Steven Holl: Berkowitz House, Martha's Vineyard, 1984. Exploded plan oblique.

carefully dismantled mechanism with all its parts shown in order of proximity and fit. The parts are shown in common orientation to each other, and although the components are not precisely aligned to the entire structure, they are laid out in proper order and sequence. It is not a representation of the building as a whole but rather a graphic synopsis of major elements and their approximate relationships.

Representing a unique way of seeing and understanding spatial relationships, axonometry has been used to symbolize an ideological position and to crystallize an architectural style. In the 1920s axonometry was vital as a symbol and tool in the development of Suprematist space and Constructivist architecture in the Soviet Union. El Lizzitsky, who presented his ideas for a new urban architecture, Sky Hook, in drawings like Figure 3.11, first formulated and promoted the manifesto of the Suprematist model of space in his essay "Architecture and Pangeometry." Therein he declared: "Suprematism has shifted

Figure 3.11 El Lissitzky. Sky Hook
project, aerial view, 1924. Axonometric.

the top of the finite pyramid of perspective vision into infin-
ity . . . " (Lissitzky 1970, 145). The station point of perspective describes a specific, fixed point from which visual rays
emanate, defining a "finite pyramid." In comparison, the visual
construction rays of axonometry are parallel, vanishing to no
point or to a point located infinitely far away. Perspective has a
center of construction, the station point; the axonometric has no
equivalent. Rather, the construction is spatially non-hierarchi-
cal, which appealed to the ideological stance of the Suprematists.

All treatises preceding [the advent of the modern use of axonometry
(1923)]. . . emphasize the convenience and accuracy of axonometry
whereas the modern celebrated its perceptive ambiguity; thus
Lissitzky's concern for the virtual expansibility of axonometric
vanishing lines into the foreground as well as in depth. The
axonometric image is reversible; it tears free of the ground
[Malevich's term], facilitating aerial views . . . Aiming to destroy the
supremacy of the facade, the architects of modernity concentrated on
this reversibility, depicting their buildings sometimes from above,
sometimes from below, and using space in which foreground and
background are exchangeable (Bois 1981, 56–57).

For them, the axonometric construct manifested this spatial
idea through the manner that the construction remains constant

throughout the drawing, having no variance for viewer or object position. Therefore the form as well as the process of the drawing spoke about the form of their ideas. That is, the drawing construction was important to them not just as a depictive format but as a quotient of meaning as well.[4] As symbolic of their polemical position, it was opposed to the hierarchical order of classicism and the emphasis on facade. Instead, they strived for an architecture which could have an equivalency of elements in space, no front, back or sides, no near or far, top or bottom, major or minor, no interior or exterior.[5] Space was to be neutral, amorphous, infinite, and the axonometric drawing form reinforced this sense of infinite extension. The Suprematists had almost no hope of building their projects and, in that sense, their drawings are almost purely rhetorical. Drawings were their end product, that is, drawings were the final construction, their architecture. They were not a means to a building but to a realized image. Stirling's and Holl's drawings, however, serve a dual purpose as representative of shapes meant to be built as well as a drawing type symbolic of a viewpoint and view of architecture.

Axonometry symbolizes accuracy and clarity in representation as well as simply depicting shapes and relationships in graphic space. But even without the symbolic connotations, axonometric constructs provide designers with a convenient tool with which to model three-dimensional complexity. The facsimile of three-dimensionality combined with the ease of construction and scaling make it a compelling graphic device with which to study developing designs from many viewpoints and with virtually any degree of dissection.

Explanatory Note: Axonometric Drawing

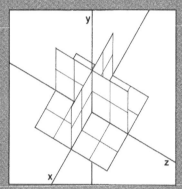

Figure 3.B1

Axonometry = axono + metry or axis measure. Axonometric drawings use three axes of length (x), width (z), and height (y) for measurement (Figure 3.B1). Using these three measuring lines (or measurements along lines anywhere in the drawing parallel to those three axes), planes with dimensions along axes x and y (length and height), axes z and y (width and height), and axes x and z (length and width) can be drawn. In this way, axonometrics are literally three-dimensional in the manner that dimensions are measured along three directions. In comparison, plans, sections, or elevations indicate two dimensions in each construction.

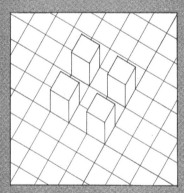

Figure 3.B2

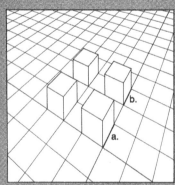

Figure 3.B3

Axonometrics retain consistent scalar measurements parallel to the three axes. Measurement remains absolute rather than the relative dimensions of the perspective. Also lines parallel in the object remain parallel in the drawing in axonometric constructions, making the drawing easier to construct than a perspective drawing. As there is no diminishment in size as the object "recedes," parts of the building shown farther away remain the same size as those in the foreground, making it easier to retain the same level of detail and information throughout the graphic (Figure 3.B2). Forms of the same size at different locations stay the same shape and size. In contrast, perspective, the other commonly used drawing construction which shows three dimensions, shows parallel lines in the object tapering toward a vanishing point (Figure 3.B3). It requires much more intricate construction and calculation. Unit measurements along the measuring lines vary dependent on location in the drawing. Thus, for example, line segment a and b in Figure 3.B3 have a different measured length even though they indicate an equal length in the object.

In a type of axonometric projection called oblique, an orthographic drawing (plan, section, or elevation) is used as a base drawing. If the plan is used as the base, height is added, creating the plan oblique (Figure 3.B4a). If the elevation is used as the base, depth is added, creating the elevation oblique (Figure 3.B4b). A section can be used as the base, creating the section oblique. Drawings can also be used in combination, such as a plan/elevation oblique. In addition, a plan oblique can cut through the building showing a sectional condition.

In the second major type of axonometric called isometric (iso + metric = equal measure), an orthographic projection cannot be used as a base drawing. Rather the plan must be redrawn using three axes separated equally by 120° (Figure 3.B5). Height along axis y is then given similar to the plan oblique. The resultant drawing suggests a viewpoint lower than the plan oblique and most closely resembles a perspective drawing of the object drawn from a great distance.

Finally, a third type of axonometric consists of those drawings that show a view from below the object, looking upward. These drawings are commonly called "worm's-eye views," up views, or Choisy axonometrics (Figure 3.B6). As the drawing shows a view from the bottom up, the construction reveals the underside of surfaces such as ceilings or soffits in relationship to walls instead of the top side of surfaces, such as floors or roofs, which are shown by the down views of the plan oblique. Up views can be drawn in any axonometric construction (elevation oblique, isometric, etc.)

The convenience of construction of the axonometric drawing is a major advantage. As dimensional measure, parallelism, and orthogonality stay consistent throughout, the drawing is relatively easy and quick to construct. Its convenience and rendition of three dimensions allow for rapid visualization, explication to self and others, and therefore establishes its value as a design method and presentation tool.

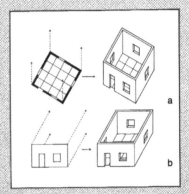

Figure 3.B4

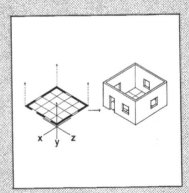

Figure 3.B5

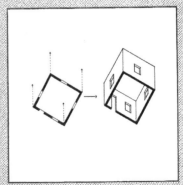

Figure 3.B6

Chapter 4

Perspective Drawings

Refer to the Explanatory Note at the end of this chapter for specific information on the conventions of perspective drawings.

As the axonometric drawing "orients itself toward the object," the **perspective** orients to the viewer, depicting the specific viewpoint of an individual and thereby highlighting the relativity of visual perception.[1] This specificity is the key to the perspective, both the source of its power as well as its liability. It creates an intense illusion of "being there" at the expense of the convenience and uniformity of paraline graphic models. The viewing position is clearly located by a perspective drawing, such that one is able to find the exact spot on a site that allows one to see the lines of a building as represented by the lines of a drawing.

Two drawings by the office of Frank Lloyd Wright for the National Life Insurance Company Office Building project of 1924 illustrate the differences between axonometry and perspective, the two drawing types that depict three dimensions. Although drawn with the same orientation, their results are strikingly different. In the axonometric view (Figure 4.1), sets of lines remain parallel throughout the drawing and measure is consistent and absolute along three axes. Knowing the scale, one could measure dimensions anywhere within the plate. Shapes and angles also remain constant. The format allows one to quickly grasp volumetric relationships: four equal wings abut a linear spine to which two taller barlike shapes are attached; a base element of one story height is shown in the gaps between the four bars; the top is highly articulated. The four projecting wings are drawn identically.

Figure 4.1 Frank Lloyd Wright: National Life Insurance Company Office Building Project, Chicago, Illinois, 1924. Plan Oblique. Ink on art paper, 46″ × 36″. (Courtesy of The Frank Lloyd Wright Archives. Copyright © The Frank Lloyd Wright Foundation 1955).

However, in the perspective drawing of the same project (Figure 4.2), shapes, dimensions and angles are relative and variable throughout the drawing, making it extremely difficult to use as a measure. For example, here the four wings do not have equal sizes or shapes and it is impossible to know whether the building is organized on a 90- or an 83- or a 72-degree system as angles cannot be measured. Vertical lines in the drawing remain parallel, but lines describing horizontal conditions slope downward to the right and left. They are *foreshortened*, angling toward vanishing points and not drawn parallel.

Figure 4.2 Frank Lloyd Wright: National Life Insurance Company Office Building Project, Chicago, Illinois, 1924. Perspective. Pencil on trace, 24″ × 18″. (Courtesy of The Frank Lloyd Wright Archives. Copyright © The Frank Lloyd Wright Foundation 1942).

Some shapes are not as visible as in the axonometric: The one-story base is hidden; the projection of the two taller barlike shapes at the back of the building is not seen; the depth of the gaps between the four wings is ambiguous.

However, although this spatial relativity makes the perspective drawing more time consuming to construct and more difficult to use as a device for measuring of dimensions and shapes than the axonometric, it is also the basis of the drawing's most distinctive and valuable characteristic. That is, since its construction is dependent on the location of a presumed viewer, the drawing is relative to a location and depicts the nature of a view from one spot. It creates an illusion of standing at that place, looking at the project. Every different *station point*, or the point from which the view is taken, will produce a different picture. In this case the drawing is constructed by projecting lines from a point representing a view slightly above sidewalk height diagonally across from the main corner. Projecting lines from a different point, left or right, closer or farther, higher or lower, will alter the result. But this is how perspective creates a semblance of vision. When one faces an object obliquely, there are no consistent measures of length and width, angularity and parallelism. There is, instead, the constantly adjusting view as one gets closer and farther and moves around and through a building. Viewing from above, from below, or to one side has its own special characteristics, the product of seeing at once vertical planes in relationship to each other along with horizontal conditions in a changing set of visual relationships. In the perspective drawing, depth, length, and width are all shown, relative to each other, and most importantly, relative to a specific viewing point. A photograph taken from the specified station point of the drawing will closely resemble the drawing. Compare, for example, Figure 4.3, a perspective drawing of Fallingwater, the Kaufmann House at Bear Run, Pennsylvania, to Figure 4.4, a photograph taken from a spot close to the station point of the drawing.

Figure 4.3 Frank Lloyd Wright: Kaufmann House, Mill Run, Pennsylvania, 1935. Perspective. Pencil and colored pencil on trace, 17″ × 33″. (Courtesy of The Frank Lloyd Wright Archives. Copyright © The Frank Lloyd Wright Foundation 1959).

Figure 4.4 Frank Lloyd Wright:
Kaufmann House, Mill Run,
Pennsylvania, 1935. (Hedrich-Blessing
photograph courtesy the Chicago
Historical Society).

The office of Frank Lloyd Wright used perspective drawings as a key element of their working methods because of this capability to depict an immmediate sense of viewing from a specific spot. They rarely used three-dimensional models, instead preferring to use the two-dimensional models of plan, section, and elevation supplemented by the spatiality of the perspective. Carefully choosing views and drawing angles to analyze critical aspects of their designs, they selected a variety of viewpoints to focus on issues such as mass, enclosed space, relationships of elements, or placement in the land. Sometimes they drew two or three views of the same building, in order to test more completely a proposal. These drawings served as a means to refine, develop, and confirm Wright's ideas.[2]

Three perspective drawings of the Avery Coonley house (Figures 4.5–4.7), using **aerial, eye level,** and **interior** viewpoints, show Wright's use of drawings done from various viewpoints in order to test three-dimensional conceptions. He often used aerial views when the project was such that an eye level construction would not allow a sufficient view of the entirety, such as projects with courtyards, several extended wings, or L-shaped plans. In these cases the station point was raised to allow a view over the forward masses and to receive a better sense of the space/mass relationships. For example, in Figure 4.5, the aerial perspective clarifies the joining of masses, the spaces they define, and their relationship to the manipulations of the ground plane. The size and depth of the pool are also indicated in this raised view, as is the nature of particular

Figure 4.5 Frank Lloyd Wright: Avery Coonley House, Riverside, Illinois, 1907. Perspective. (Courtesy of The Frank Lloyd Wright Archives. Copyright © The Frank Lloyd Wright Foundation 1962).

intersections between the central mass and the continuous link. Although most of the lines of the building are ruled, areas of freehand drawing indicate changes and adjustments as the drawing progresses, for example in the small projecting wing on the far right side.

In contrast to the sense of an observer hovering above the building, Figure 4.6 uses an eye level viewpoint to create an illusion of standing close to the house, viewing the structure through a screen of trees. The drawing gives a sense of immediacy, of being there, depicting the quality of experiencing the house from that place. However, the eye level view makes it more difficult to determine the width and depth of the pool, and the masses behind are invisible in this drawing. Though ruled and accurately constructed, this perspective is also used to study changes to the design. For example, it appears that the addition of a chimney mass was tentatively tested, indicated by the lightly sketched mass at the pavilion's peak, which was in turn added definitively to the house in later drawings. In addition, a chimney and a raised lantern are erased at the mass on the right and also eliminated in the aerial view.

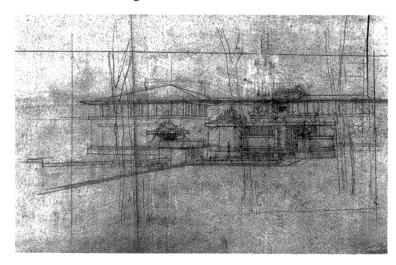

Figure 4.6 Frank Lloyd Wright: Avery Coonley House, Riverside, Illinois, 1907. Perspective. (Courtesy of The Frank Lloyd Wright Archives. Copyright © The Frank Lloyd Wright Foundation 1985).

However, though those changes are accommodated in the aerial drawing and in the final project, even the aerial drawing does not show the eventual final design as a pergola was added across the front of the central pavilion and a trellis element was added to articulate the roof and front of the same mass.

The third study drawing of the Coonley house (Figure 4.7) shows the living room interior. This ruled and carefully constructed drawing shows furniture and lighting fixtures added in freehand. However, one important architectural feature is also drawn freehand, suggesting a design change stimulated by the view of the perspective: At the base of the vaulted ceiling an area of grillwork is sketched in between ceiling moldings. This grillwork serves to ornament and conceal artificial lighting fixtures and was eventually incorporated into the final design.

Figure 4.7 Frank Lloyd Wright: Avery Coonley House, Riverside, Illinois, 1907. Perspective. (Courtesy of The Frank Lloyd Wright Archives. Copyright © The Frank Lloyd Wright Foundation 1985).

Wright often relied on and tested project revisions in sketches drawn over carefully measured, meticulously accurate hardline drawings constructed by draftspersons in his office. However, he also used freehand, sketchy *thumbnail drawings* to help formulate the beginning concepts of a project. Thumbnail refers to their small size, often on the order of two or three inches square. This format allows for a type of graphic shorthand, an economy of expression where one can strike a few lines to depict rapidly and laconically the essential elements of a scheme. A single line in these small drawings can represent an architectural element such as a pier, column, or row of windows. In Wright's thumbnail sketch of the Imperial Hotel in Tokyo, Japan (Figure 4.8), one can see the testing of ideas in a distinctively cryptic manner: A few dark lines indicate a colonnande or a row of deeply recessed piers; an area of white indicates a recessed mass; a series of vertical lines on the flanking wings indicate a pattern of windows. Through this small quick sketch one is able to grasp the essential features of his concept: long parallel flanking wings, an entry forecourt with entrance pavilion, connecting wings and at the end of the axis the dominant "head" piece. Heavier line weights and repetitive lines emphasize critical places in the design.

Figure 4.8 Frank Lloyd Wright: Imperial Hotel, Tokyo. 1914. Perspective. (Courtesy of The Frank Lloyd Wright Archives. Copyright © The Frank Lloyd Wright Foundation 1985).

Wright's use of perspective drawings to check his three dimensional conceptualizations is further shown by the sequence of the design for the Kaufmann House, also known as Fallingwater. There are different accounts of the way that he began work on this project, but it is generally accepted that Wright was thinking of the commission for nine months before he began any drawings in the office, and he evidently started those drawings only a few hours before the arrival of Kaufmann for their first meeting on the house (in perhaps an extreme example of architectural procrastination).[3] He began by rapidly preparing a set of orthographic drawings, executing the plans, a transverse section, and south elevation within a few hours. The plan (Figure 4.9) is a uniquely three-dimensional expression of the building, a composite of all three of its levels. It depicts the stone and concrete supports at the base level (thick *pochéd*

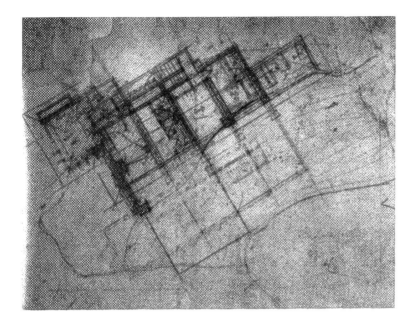

Figure 4.9 Frank Lloyd Wright: Kaufmann House, Mill Run, Pennsylvania, 1935. Plan. Pencil and colored pencil on trace. (Courtesy of The Frank Lloyd Wright Archives. Copyright © The Frank Lloyd Wright Foundation 1959).

walls); light hardlines indicate the living room level with its stair to the water below; and freehand sketched lines describe the upper bedroom level. Color differentiates the floors: the upper floor is coded with sepia-colored pencil; blue-gray *poché* walls signify the lowest foundation level, and blue-gray lines without *poché* the living level. As a synoptic graphic synthesizing all levels, the drawing coordinates the building three-dimensionally, a formal and conceptual layering of the imagined structure, allowing Wright to visualize structural relationships, horizontal and vertical circulation, even plumbing locations. The south elevation (Figure 4.10) reveals the long horizontal striations of the building to be a reiteration of the line of the waterfall and of the rock strata upon which the foundations were to sit. The drawing is wonderfully evocative in the manner that window patterns have been drawn and partially erased, that lines vary in weight and intensity as they move across horizontally, that shadows are so subtle as to read similarly to the patterns of stone in light, and in the way that planes seem to recede and advance, compressing the series of planes into a pattern of lines, all tying the building to the abstracted line of the waterfall itself.

Following his meeting with Kaufmann, two of Wright's apprentices worked through the night constructing perspectives, an aerial and eye level drawing.[4] These drawings (Figures 4.11 and 4.12) have slightly different station point locations in plan, but the biggest difference is in the height of their viewing points, resulting in two plates of very different effects and

Figure 4.10 Frank Lloyd Wright: Kaufmann House, Mill Run, Pennsylvania, 1935. Elevation. Pencil, colored pencil on trace. (Courtesy of The Frank Lloyd Wright Archives. Copyright © The Frank Lloyd Wright Foundation 1959).

Figure 4.11 Frank Lloyd Wright: Kaufmann House, Mill Run, Pennsylvania, 1935. Perspective. Pencil, colored pencil. (Courtesy of The Frank Lloyd Wright Archives. Copyright © The Frank Lloyd Wright Foundation 1962).

Figure 4.12 Frank Lloyd Wright:
Kaufmann House, Mill Run,
Pennsylvania, 1935. Perspective.
(Courtesy of The Frank Lloyd Wright
Archives. Copyright © The Frank Lloyd
Wright Foundation 1962).

efficacy. The aerial drawing establishes clearly the vertical and horizontal relationships between floors and concrete slabs, illustrating the particular manner that slabs overlap in alternating directions, so that how the building fits together is precisely represented. The other drawing positions the view approximately at the base of the waterfall, looking up at the house, seeing much of the underside of the concrete slabs. The drawing dramatizes the visual presence of the living room slab when viewed from below, leaving a viewer with a vivid impression of its visual impact as seen from that point of the site.

Although these perspectives followed the plans, elevation, and section drawings that Wright had prepared, their role in his conceptual process was not after the fact. After four decades of practice, Wright had a remarkable capability to visualize a project in his mind, in essence to be able to see the drawings of the project in his imagination. In his words, "I *no longer* touch pencil to paper until the idea of the design is so fixed within my own imagination that I am arranging the furniture and placing bowls of flowers within the building. Then I go to paper and put it down [emphasis provided]" (Futagawa 1985, viii). This ability is demonstrated by the development of this project where the basic forms of the house had been set by the time the orthographic drawings were completed. Perspectives then served as a means to confirm the major decisions and to study minor refinements and changes to the design. He made changes, even after the preparation of the finished colored perspective used for publication (Figure 4.3). He increased the height of the main chimney, added a thin cantilever slab over the windows of the living room, and extended the concrete

Figure 4.13 Mies van der Rohe, Ludwig: Hubbe house, 1935. Perspective of living room and court. Pencil on illustration board, 19″ × 26½″. (Collection, Mies van der Rohe Archive, The Museum of Modern Art, New York. Gift of the architect).

fascia of the main floor terrace back onto the face of the stone wall (compare Figure 4.3 with the photograph of the finished house, Figure 4.4). The perspectives served a key role in depicting these kinds of formal relationships.

Even though the drawing records of Mies van der Rohe are dominated by plan studies, his perspectives, while far fewer in number, served as critical tests of his vision, enabling him to see subtle spatial relationships only schematically mapped out in plans. Two perspectives of the Hubbe House (Figures 4.13 and 4.14) articulate the same space with dramatically different effects. While both drawings depict a powerfully simple strategy for making space, one is drawn precisely, testing details and specifics while the other is general and impulsive. In both drawings, horizontal elements are powerful presences, yet they are only suggested, not made explicit. One assumes that a ceiling hovers overhead, although it is indicated only through the absence of tone or mark. It is the vertical elements, wall planes, columns, furniture, trees, and sculpture, which are drawn and positioned between the hovering ceiling and ground plane. The difference in the two drawings indicates the difference in motivation and viewpoint. The first drawing (Figure 4.13) has been laid out with care and accuracy. A vanishing point has been precisely located and all receding lines converge directly on it. Though the drawing employs some rapid freehand scrawls, the carefully crafted outlines indicate that the drawing was sketched over a hardline base. It is a drawing used to study precise relationships and proportions, even the effect of furniture placement and size on the spatial composition. In comparison, the second drawing (Figure 4.14)

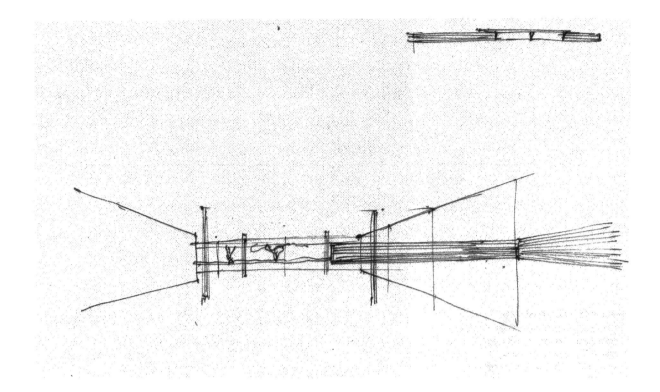

Figure 4.14 Mies van der Rohe, Ludwig: Hubbe house, 1935. Interior perspective and elevation sketches. Ink on tracing, 8¼″ × 11¾″. (Collection, Mies van der Rohe Archive, The Museum of Modern Art, New York. Gift of the architect).

displays a much less controlled, more impulsive attitude. Accuracy appears to be less important than speed, as if Mies were concerned with seeing the essentials of the space, not its details: The proportions of the garden wall are greatly distorted (almost twice its actual length); the columns are brought into the glazed enclosure; and the vanishing point is vaguely positioned and inconsistently used. Done freehand without a constructed underlay, the drawing is intense, terse, and far less accurate.

Perspective sketches were the key drawings for Erich Mendelsohn. "Look at my sketch," he said, "there is everything in it" (Whittick 1956, 11). He was in the habit of studying a problem for a period of time and in an intense concentrated moment, described as an "outpouring," would execute a series of small perspectives on a single sheet, sometimes as many as twenty or thirty. Each of these sketches is a thumbnail study, a completed entity in itself, where rather than correcting or changing a drawing, he rapidly executed another one. These multiple drawings present a set of alternatives, rapidly and spontaneously drawn, a display of possibilities to himself. A set of sketches for an office building in Berlin (Figure 4.15) shows the building mass and form. The drawings are freehand, done without plan construction, and indicate little detail, being comprised of quick, confident lines. The effect is to make the

Figure 4.15 Eric Mendelsohn:
Administration Building of the German
Metalworkers Union, Berlin, 1929.
Perspectives. Pencil on trace,
14½″ × 14″. (Staatliche Museen zu
Berlin, Kunstbibliothek).

buildings appear heroic and monumental. Scale is unclear, made ambiguous by a horizon line set slightly *below* ground level. The observer is required to look up, endowing the respective project with a powerful, larger-than-life presence. In addition, Mendelsohn's consistent use of two-point perspectival viewpoints emphasizes the nature of the corner with one side vanishing left, the other right, which, combined with his exaggerated, elongated treatment of building proportion and shape and the sweeping motion of line and surface articulation, gives his drawings a powerful sense of movement.

The typical interior perspective view creates the illusion of being in a space. In this **section perspective** of the Yale School of Architecture by Paul Rudolph (Figure 4.16), the spatial depth of perspective is combined with the unique view provided by a sectional cut. The highly textured drawing opens up the building by slicing across its main interior spaces, revealing the relationships of large and small, contained and flowing. At the same time it shows in a direct and straightforward way the relationships between interior spaces and exterior form and in the process gives information about the fabric of the building: its structural strategy, its enclosure, its material, even its ductwork. All this is revealed in the drawing essentially due to

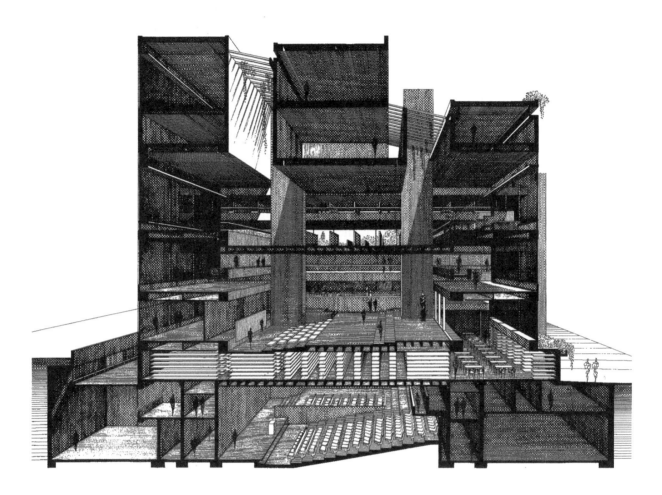

Figure 4.16 Paul Rudolph: Yale School of Architecture, New Haven, Connecticut. Section perspective. Ink.

its sectional format but, as a perspective, it reveals this information in an enhanced way, in depth. The experience of a viewer positioned at a fixed location and looking into the opened building is enhanced by the spatial depth of perspective. The vanishing point is set at a point horizontal with the eye level of the occupants located on the mezzanine balcony, which overlooks the central public commons. The result is that the structure is divided by a horizon line (emphasized by the mid-building floor which separates the top half of the building from the lower), which gives the combined effect of an up view/down view. Thus the experience of each individual space is compared with the unique experience of simultaneously seeing into each space at every level. This sense of standing in the building is further strengthened through the graphic treatment of light and materiality. Light streaming through the windows and skylights creates rhythms and patterns of shade and shadow that emphasize the rough concrete texture of the interior surfaces. Dense and painstakingly drafted hatched lines render the textures of the horizontal and vertical surfaces, which confirm their planar orientation and reinforce at every point the perspectival sensation.

Perspective is more than just a drawing type or convention of representation, as it also serves to symbolize the ideals of an era. During the Renaissance, perspective was not only a representation of architecture, but also a method of seeing or understanding the world, in short, a world view. It represented a way of knowing, a system that defined the relationship of things in space. Through this system one could conceive a project, then model the perception of it through perspective. The ability to model perception meant that one could in effect predict the future, an empowering capability congruent with the aspirations of the age, the idea of human beings taking responsibility for the outcome of things. The power of perspective construction rests in its linear, precise, and rational nature. It is authoritative in the manner that its techniques appear scientific, that is, systematic and verifiable.[5]

Jorge Silvetti proposes that in the Renaissance there developed a *cultural format* within which perspective played a central symbolic role:

. . . a very unique format where an ideology, a conception of space, an architectural language, a newly defined practice (architecture), and a political structure all coincided and found their best, most felicitous and synthetic symbol in the newly "discovered" technique of illusionistic representation of three dimensional space in two dimensions (Silvetti 1984, p. 14).

Perspective as a "symbolic form" bound a method of drawing construction with the humanistic ideals of the Renaissance. This drawing construct came to represent both the specific architectural content of its lines as well as an entire mode of seeing and ordering the world. That is, these drawings were seen as incorporating an ideological framework. The architects of the Renaissance chose perspective construction as an important tool to make as well as symbolize their architecture. A drawing method transcended its role as medium and instead became, in a way, an end in itself.

The axiality of the **one-point** perspectival construction of the late-fifteenth century painting *View of an Ideal City* (Figure 4.17) manifests the congruence between the axial organization of Renaissance architecture and the perspective mode of representation. As Silvetti puts it: "With this type of perspective

Figure 4.17 Central Italian School, late fifteenth century: "View of an Ideal City." Perspective. 30″ × 56½″. (Walters Art Gallery, Baltimore, Maryland).

which puts us in the center of the world from where everything is viewed, analyzed, measured and known, the ideological apparatus of humanism encounters its most felicitous symbolic form" (Silvetti 1982, p. 171). The one point perspective view conventionalized during the Renaissance aligns the line of sight with either the x or z planes of an orthogonal object. Sight is parallel to architecture in a manner that allows a vanishing point to occur essentially in the center of vision (Figure 4.B5, page 79). The center of view is demarcated by a point to which a series of perspectival lines lead. In this drawing construction then, the centrality of view is reinforced by a formal center of the drawing that locates and emphasizes the viewer's presence and importance.

As perspectival representation during the Renaissance was dominated by the centrality and axiality of one point perspective, representation during the Baroque period was influenced by two **point perspective** and its ability to establish a non-centered view.[6] Since lines do not lead to a single point present within the frame but rather to points left and right, sometimes with equal emphasis, sometimes weighted in one direction or the other, the viewer is tugged between two points, and the outside or inside corners of the objects confronting him or her resist static occupancy (Figure 4.18). In one-point perspective drawings, the viewer's gaze is readily drawn into the image along the diagonal lines of recession. A sense of closure results. In the two point drawing there is no single end point and resultant sense of finality. Rather, the opposing diagonality of the drawing can be exploited to create continuous, unclosed volumes, as was so powerfully done by Piranesi (see Figure 9.1).

Figure 4.18 Ferdinando Galli Bibiena: "Drawing of a stage design." Perspective. (Courtesy of the British Museum).

The idealized vision of a drawing affects vision itself by changing conceptions of what one experiences. Perspective is not a mirror of reality.[7] It seemingly gives an exact replication of what one would see if one were standing in front of the object. However, it differs in important ways from vision: Perspective is monocular and therefore presents a fixed view with a uniformly clear, focused picture rather than the reality of binocular visual perception with its constantly adjusting focal depths, areas of attention and clarity; and perspective's construction is based on the premise of a flat picture plane, which results in distortions of shapes at the edges of the drawing, as compared to vision and the curved receiving surface of the retina. Perspectival representation does not depict a reality identical to human vision (neither does a photograph), but the belief that perspective and vision are the same leads to expectations which blur the differences between the two. That is, the perception of persons versed in perspectival techniques and familiar with the drawings tend to be influenced by its results. Thus the straight line constructs of a perspective drawing tend to cause an expectation of sight which hinders one from noticing the gentle curvature seen in actual straight line conditions as a result of the concavity of the retina. In addition, perspective necessarily works to a closed frame, which is often described as the area of distortion-free, focused view. However, human visual capacities include a cone of view generally exceeding 180 degrees when peripheral vision is included but only a narrow area of sharp, focused vision of 10 degrees.[8] When compared to this dynamic focal possibility, the frame of a drawing seems to be an arbitrary point of closure. Some drawings try to compensate for this limitation. For example, in his aerial drawing of Cranbrook (Figure 4.19), Eliel Saarinen gives a semblance of the characteristics of focused and peripheral vision by reducing the degree of resolution on the perimeter of the drawing: Pencil strokes become coarser with more visible marks and short erased areas bring the white of the paper through the deep tone. Thus the drawing attempts to compensate for the way that perspective differs from the nature of vision.[9]

As can be seen from this discussion, perspective, this most "lifelike" of drawing constructions, is exactly that—like life, but different. A drawing constructs a world seen, distorting and shaping vision to fit its shape. The effects of perspective point out the inevitable and necessary effect of all drawing: There is a distance between the representation and what it attempts to represent. Perspective, like all drawings, is an idealized, abstracted form of vision, which, by freezing sight, emphasizes the view from a singular point in space and encourages a "solution" from that view. Finally, this drawing construction, by presenting a particular way of seeing, changes perception, making one look at the world through the filter of perspective.

Figure 4.19 Eliel Saarinen (1873–1950): Aerial View of Cranbrook School, Bloomfield Hills, Michigan, 1926. Perspective. Pencil on paper, 21½″ × 25⅜″. (Collection of Cranbrook Academy of Art Museum, CAAM 1954.5).

Explanatory Note: Perspective Drawing

Figure 4.B1 Albrecht Dürer: "A draughtsman drawing a portrait," c. 1525. Perspective. Woodcut, 5¼" × 5¼". (Courtesy of the Victoria & Albert Museum).

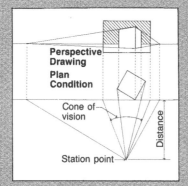

Figure 4.B2

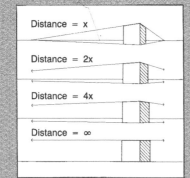

Figure 4.B3

Perspective can be defined as the plotting of points seen through a transparent plane from a specified point and is described by its Latin root, perspectus, *or looking through (Figure 4.B1).*

The diagram of the method of perspective construction called plan projection, Figure 4.B2, illustrates the variables that influence the look and tone of the resultant drawing. These are all related to the condition of the viewing subject, that is, the location of the viewer relative to the object (called the station point) and the width of the view. These variables stated briefly and explained below more fully are: distance of viewer from the object; angle of the viewer relative to the surfaces of the object; height of the viewer relative to the height of the object; and the width of the view (called the cone of vision). All of these dramatically affect the appearance of the drawing.

For example, in Figure 4.B3, the shapes of the cubes vary as the distance of the viewer from the object varies. The closer the viewer is located, the steeper the angle of vanishing lines. As the viewer moves farther and farther away from the object, the angle of the lines flattens and approaches horizontal. Eventually, for vanishing points located infinitely far away, the horizontal surfaces of the object remain horizontal in the drawing, producing an elevation view.

The second variable is the angle of view relative to the surfaces of the object. In this case, shifting the viewer changes the relative amount shown of different surfaces. For example, in 4.B4a the right surface is shown relatively flat to the viewer and a great amount of the surface is seen compared to the left side of the object. In 4.B4b, both surfaces are shown aproximately equally, and in 4.B4c the left surface is shown much more. All three drawings depict the same object, but through a change of location of the viewer, the resultant representation changes the shapes and sizes of the planes and places a different emphasis on what one sees and how one sees it.

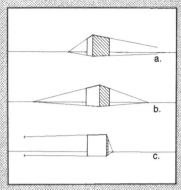

Figure 4.B4

When the line of sight is aligned parallel to one set of planes in an orthogonal building and perpendicular to the other, the resultant construction is termed a **one-point perspective** (Figure 4.B5). The drawing is distinguished by its single vanishing point and by the way that one set of horizontal and vertical lines remains parallel to a rectangular frame, establishing a formal similarity between perspective and frame. As a result, the diagonal foreshortened lines have a figural emphasis that is often stronger than in **two-point constructions**. That is, everything seems to lead to the single vanishing point with the rest of the drawing providing an effective background frame. The drawing appears as if the scene has attached itself to the frame and then been pulled back in depth with a center provided by the vanishing point.

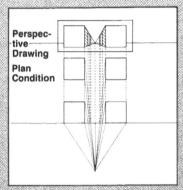

Figure 4.B5

When the height of the viewer changes relative to the height of the object, the representation also changes. In a perspective drawing, the horizon line represents the height of the station point and by implication the height of the viewer's eye. For example a 20-foot-tall cube with the viewer's eye at 5 feet high would have a horizon line located one-fourth of the way up the corner of the cube (Figure 4.B6b). Thus, 4.B6a shows a cube with a horizon line (and therefore the eye) at a height 30 feet below the base of the cube, 4.B6c shows a horizon line 30 feet above the base of the cube, and 4.B6d shows an eye height 60 feet above the base. Through the conventions of perspective, one is able to tell immediately the height of the viewer's position by comparing the horizon line location to any referent point of the object.

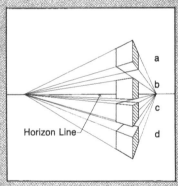

Figure 4.B6

In each perspective, the author also chooses a cone of vision, or the width and height of the view. The choice of what to include or exclude affects greatly the representational impact as the sense of context, focus, and shape are all influenced. In Figure 4.B7b, a cube is shown within a 60-degree cone of vision, which is one of the most common conventions. In 4.B7 a 120 degree cone of vision has been used, resulting in a much wider view and the inclusion of more space to the right and left of the object shown in the previous view. In 4.B7c a 20-degree cone of vision has been used resulting in a narrower, more focused view. This is a limiting of the view seen similar to the effect of a telephoto lens.

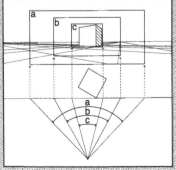

Figure 4.B7

Applications of Drawing

The first section dealt with basic drawing types. In this second section the focus is on the various ways that architects use drawing, their modes of application. This section examines the purposes, attitudes, and intentions of drawing, details the use of drawings as references of preexisting phenomena, as diagrams for analysis, for design, in order to make presentations to outsiders, and finally as a means to create visionary worlds. The book concludes with a final chapter on general issues of representation.

Chapter 7, Design Drawings, focuses on drawings used for the immediate purpose of working on a specific project. That is, the chapter collects the drawings used to study and resolve the shapes and ideas of a building design. However, the grouping and naming of these drawings as "design drawings" is admittedly an artificial distinction as we believe every drawing in this book is about architectural design. Whether drawings are referring to an existing environment, diagramming, presenting a design, or giving concrete form to a visionary idea, they pull their authors into the imaginary world of envisioning, representing, and therefore designing.

Chapter 5

Referential Drawings

In two drawings of the Athenian Acropolis one author uses flat planar tones to emphasize crisply edged masses; the other uses lyrical line work to emphasize irregularities of rock and edge. Viewing the same subject, one draws repetitive, geometrically precise walls; the other lilting profiles. Where one graphically contrasts building to land, the other joins them. Although of the same subject, the visions presented are so stylistically different as to seem to be of different places. How is it that drawings of the same subject by two authors tell such different stories?

A comparison of these drawings by Louis Kahn and Antoine Predock suggest the varied ways in which referential drawings may be used as tools to document, to see, and to design. These graphics refer to their observed views, acting as a means to record existing conditions. This is why we have chosen to use the term **referential drawings** to describe these graphics.[1] Yet these drawings also refer to their authors, presenting evidence of what and how they see through what and how they draw. A drawing is an interpretation, revealing an author's proclivities and offering evidence not only of what one chooses to draw (and therefore what one deems important enough to record), but also through the manner of drawing, the nuances of how one sees a scene. Each drawing offers clues to the perceptions of its maker, a document as particular and revealing as a signature.

In his 1951 drawing (Figure 5.1), Louis Kahn found in the Acropolis a series of regular rectilinear solids contrasted against

Figure 5.1 Louis Kahn: Acropolis, Athens, 1951. Perspective. Pastel and charcoal pencil on paper, 11 1/10″ × 14 3/5″. (Courtesy of Sue Ann Kahn).

the irregularities of the land.[2] Broad washes of pastel tone dominate this drawing, producing an effect of a series of masses, modeled in crisp sunlight, stepping across the page as if carved out of the same material. Kahn contrasts this linkage between built shapes to his treatment of the land upon which they sit. Here he has used proportionately less tone and more line work to describe irregular, uneven shapes. There is a sharp formal demarcation between built form and its setting.

Antoine Predock's drawing of a similar view (Figure 5.2) stands in stark stylistic contrast. The informalities and irregularities of the visual composition are emphasized through lyrical, irregular lines that join natural form to built form. His drawing style employs only a minimal use of tone in favor of line work. Predock smooths the edges of all built forms, presenting walls of rounded corners which merge gently with the natural cliffs of the plateau. He even draws trees at the base with dark lines similar to the lines for the columns of the Parthenon directly above. The effect depicts the architecture of the Acropolis as if it grew from and was conceptually bonded to its environment.

Figure 5.2 Antoine Predock: Acropolis, Athens, 1962. Perspective.

In making these drawings, their authors represent or re-present existing three-dimensional phenomena. Their act of representing (to others, to self) is a kind of remaking of the object. That is, as they look at the paper and attempt to "match" a line to an edge seen, they are involved in a creative condition of making a line, of deliberately establishing on paper visual relationships, such as those of proportion, light, texture, and importance. They select not only what type of drawing to structure their vision but also the angle of viewpoints, the lighting condition to show (or not to show), the proportion and scope of the view, the handling of the frame, what features to include or exclude (detail, ornamentation, profile, mass, etc.), and what to emphasize or not (shape, mass, texture, light, space, etc.). In other words, every drawing is a highly personalized editorial, an interpretation of a phenomenon, that is, an object seen by an individual and drawn by a specific hand.

In a sense these two authors rebuilt the Acropolis in their drawings. In Le Corbusier's words:

When one travels and works with visual things—architecture, painting or sculpture—one uses one's eyes and draws, so as to fix deep down in one's experience what is seen. Once the impression has been recorded by the pencil, it stays for good, entered, registered, inscribed . . . To draw oneself, to trace the lines, handle the volumes, organize the surface . . . all this means first to look, and then to observe and finally perhaps to discover . . . and it is then that inspiration may come. Inventing, creating, one's whole being is drawn into action, and it is this action which counts (Le Corbusier 1960, p. 37).

The act of representation requires this "rebuilding," or remaking on paper that Le Corbusier believes is "to handle the volumes, organize the surface . . ." His statement is quite literal, not in terms of handling the volumes or organizing the surface of the object *seen*, but in terms of the physical manipulation of the object *drawn*. One organizes the object on paper, adjusting lines, giving it shape, materiality, texture, volume. The building is raised from the ground of the paper.

When one works on a referential drawing, one experiences a double phenomenon, confronting the subject being drawn and the drawing as a restatement of that subject. This dual experience changes the nature of the interaction between author and subject. The act of drawing requires a more conscious recognition of shapes such as details, proportions, and configurations, enhancing the author's cognitive awareness of specifics.

The drawings of Kahn and Predock are both perspectival, that is, views taken from a specific point. However, references can be drawn using any drawing type, media, or be done for many different purposes. Referential drawings can be orthographic, perspectival, or axonometric drawings, done with pastel, charcoal, or ink, as a means to an end or an end in themselves. What distinguishes them from the other applications of drawing is their focus on existing phenomena and their intent to draw that which is seen, to use a drawing as a means of understanding what is in order to design what might be.

In his pen and ink sketch of the Medici Chapel in Florence, Eugene Mackey, Jr. (Figure 5.3) uses orthographic and axonometric projections in order to depict and understand its formal organization undistorted by the perceptual viewpoint of perspective. He records the shapes, positions, relationships, and dimensions in an unembellished and abstract manner. The plan and section drawings give considerable detail about surface treatment, location of niches, alcoves, pilasters, and dimensions and proportions of the space, while the axonometric view simplifies the configuration of pendentives which fit the dome

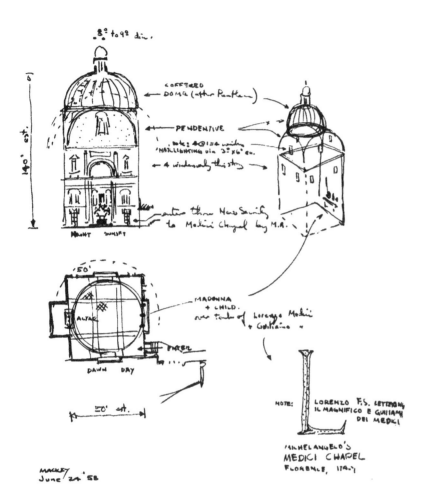

Figure 5.3 Eugene Mackey, Jr.: Medici Chapel, Florence, 1958. Plan, section, isometric. Ink on paper. (Eugene Mackey, FAIA).

to the square shaft of space below. These amalgamations of separate incremental observations are coordinated and related through the format of the sheet. Finally, he uses notes to confirm dimensions, label niche contents, describe the access route, and comment on comparisons, "coffered dome (after Pantheon)."

In his travel sketches, Fumihiko Maki often sketches plans and sections as a means to organize and structure his thoughtful observations. Typical of these carefully composed orthographic drawings, which are filled with fine sure lines and notes of description and impressions, is his sketch of the courtyard of a small hotel encountered on the way to Venice (Figure 5.4). He lays out the placement and proportions of the elements: columns, their spacing and alignment, the paths of circulation in the location of stairs and entry, and the position of mezzanines and balconies overhead. The adjacent section drawing marks out the vertical configuration of the stairs and the size and

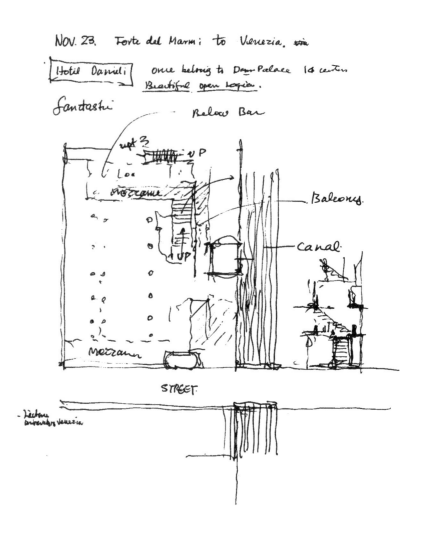

Figure 5.4 Fumihiko Maki: Hotel Danieli, Venice. Plan, section.

position of the aperture through the thick wall allowing for cross-reference with the plan and providing vertical information about the space.

Caroline Mauduit records her yearlong travels and studies in *An Architect in Italy,* a lovingly crafted book full of gentle, richly colored watercolor sketches. The author uses drawings both to record accurate measurements and depictions of the dimensions and proportions of the facade as well as to represent their coloration and textural sense through watercolor wash. About such drawings, she said: "Often I measured it and made a plan, putting the dimensions on the drawing, because I know from experience that only by doing that can I understand what I am looking at." One page depicts her study of Vignola's facade for the Palazzo dei Banchi in Bologna in a series of elevations (Figure 5.5). The bay segment studies on the right side provide detailed information, revealing the texture of materials, volu-

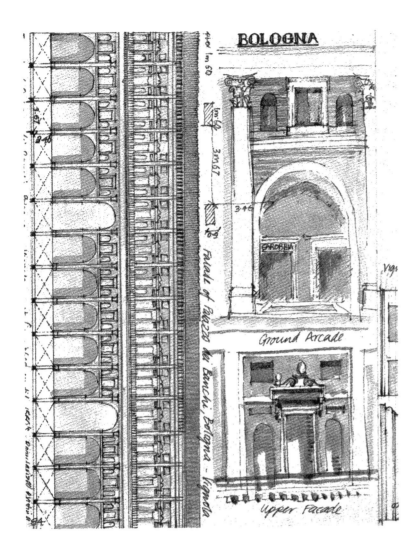

Figure 5.5 Caroline Mauduit: Palazzo dei Banchi, Bologna, 1984. Plan, elevation. (From *An Architect in Italy* by Caroline Mauduit. Copyright © 1988 by Caroline Mauduit. Reprinted by permission of Clarkson N. Potter, Inc., a division of Crown Publishers, Inc.).

metric depth (implied through shadow), and enough detail of the carved stone configuration to presume the style of the column's order. Though the upper drawing is basically a standard elevation, the depth of the portico bay is suggested by the artifice of imposed perspective. The drawing provides enough spatial and detail information to give the viewer an impression of standing in the street looking at the facade. By comparison, the upturned elevation running the length of the left edge of the page gives a much more coherent impression of the facade as a whole by drawing it at a substantially smaller scale and showing at least fifteen bays of the facade. A plan grafted to the bottom of the elevation accurately describes the depth of the portico. Finally, the portico's dimensions are indicated in a diagram in the middle upper portion.

Figure 5.6 Isadore Shank: Le Petit Trianon, Versailles, 1919. Elevation. Pencil, ink and ink wash on board, 14″ × 29½″.

Figure 5.7 Jane Pelton: Angkor Wat, Cambodia, 1928. Perspective. Pencil on paper.

Isadore Shank's study of the Le Petit Trianon at Versailles, France (Figure 5.6), demonstrates his training in the Beaux Arts tradition of nineteenth century architectural pedagogy wherein designated monuments were examined and drawn as a means to study composition and proportion as well as practice draftsmanship. As an academic exercise, Shank is concerned with the precise position and relationship of every part. The shape and proportion of each element of the facade is drawn carefully and accurately. Elevation views such as this typically have no mechanism for explicitly depicting the third dimension. Yet through the author's painstaking effort to render light, shade, and shadow as well as the transparency of the windows and the fabrication of the masonary walls, the drawing has a strong sense of depth. The building is painstakingly drawn and rendered, constituting both a record of the structure and an independent essay of striking formal beauty.

In her drawing of Angkor Wat (Figure 5.7), Jane Pelton renders a doorway with strong and carefully crafted marks, evoking the mystery of receding interior spaces. Woven together into patterned tapestries of light and dark, the soft curlicue strokes on the lintel capture the low relief of the intricately carved ornamental stonework. Layers of darkness, defined by the crisp edges of blocks of stone glowing in sunlight, sharply define the inner walls. Veiled in a shroud of shadow, there is a vivid sense of something unknown beyond the gate, testifying to the author's sensitivity to the scene and to her control of the medium. Even the way she controlled the incompleteness of the image, carefully merging the scene with the whiteness of the page, gives the doorway an illusive presence fading in and out of view.

Louis Kahn draws the hilltown of San Gimignano, Italy, with broad strokes of a graphite stick (Figure 5.8), defining through the drawing his concern for planar solids activated by the effects of light. With an economy of marks, rapidly sketched, he describes the enclosed space of a street leading to an arched gateway, enlivened by a tower in sunlight. The graphite stick has been used directionally, building up strokes like courses of masonry, turned either horizontally or vertically.[3] The spatial effect is intense because the powerful play of bright light across the tower and its base is contrasted to a foreground defined on both sides by dark tones. The shaded side of the tower defines a sharp edge against the white of the paper. The right corner of the tower disappears, letting the space of paper enter the solid mass, merging a wall in light with a sky of bright, charging the drawing with an intensity of light, dark, solid, and void.

Figure 5.8 Louis I. Kahn: Street with a tower, San Gimignano, Italy, 1928. Perspective. Pencil on paper, 6½″ × 6⅓″. (Courtesy of Sue Ann Kahn).

Whether emphasizing process or product, architects use drawing to refer to observed scenes, as a particular mode of seeing, as a means to understand a reference in a particular way. For Le Corbusier, drawings were a kind of visual shorthand, brief, cursory jotted notes to which he frequently referred while working on projects. His sketches are explicit, formal references. For Alvar Aalto, drawing was an intuitive recording, important as an internal impression. For Bertram Goodhue, the end result is valued for its own beauty and finished condition. A comparison demonstrates how the differences in the intentions of these two architects affect both the look and the use of their drawings. Bertram Goodhue meant his drawing of Montenventoso (Figure 5.9) to be shown to an audience (in this case, intended to be published), and to be valued as a completed object. In comparison, the colleagues of Alvar Aalto have described how he stored his drawings away in drawers, unused and ignored. His emphasis on drawing from observation was not on making a finished product but on the act of recording as a particular method of seeing and experiencing:

The landscape sketches and annotations on the buildings of the past are rather a kind of spiritual exercise, a putting into practice of Aalto's basic method: to filter clearly perceived separate entities through the unconscious so that a viable synthesis arises . . . The goal is not to create artistic sketches or interesting paintings but to train the sensibilities (Schildt 1967, ix).

Figure 5.9 Bertram Goodhue: Montenventoso, Italy (published 1925). Perspective. Ink.

Aalto's drawing of Calascibetta, Italy (Figure 5.10), reveals both his concern with the relationship between building and land as well as provides a vehicle for the contemplation of place through the calligraphy of his lines. He uses the pencil in a relaxed, unself-conscious manner to restate the shapes he observed as a way to impress them into his mind. Within the dense accumulation of marks, he demarcates no single building, instead using continuous lines to create a quick impression of a tight jumble of houses. However, at a juncture between town and the surrounding landscape, Aalto concentrates on the depiction of the terraces, as if to slowly, deliberately study the transition between land and town. Here, particularities of shape *do* seem important, such as decisively drawn edges and precisely indicated details.

Figure 5.10 Alvar Aalto: Calascibetta, Italy, 1952. Perspective.

In comparison, Bertram Goodhue delineates the village of Montenventoso, Italy, with meticulous ink lines and precisely and accurately controlled detail. Like Aalto's sketch, the overall effect of the drawing is one of a dense accumulation of similar shapes, but Goodhue draws precisely specific details such as a gate with base and cornice and churches on the ridge of the hill with crosses, window patterns, and buttresses. So great is the level of detail that one expects the number of houses in a certain area of the drawing or the number of windows drawn on a certain building to correspond to the built reality. Throughout the drawing, Goodhue self-consciously manipulates tone and composition to focus on the important aspects of the scene, as when he uses dark tone on only specific parts of the mountain in order to silhouette the town. The effect is of an elegant, restrained rendition of walls in sunlight contrasted against a darker background of land.[4]

Not every referential sketch is of an existing building. Le Corbusier records his impressions of a vast variety of subjects in his sketchbooks, including bulls, rivers, landscapes, nudes, and palm fronds. These shapes and forms often reemerge in unique and unexpected ways in his later designs. Other architects draw in a similar way and for the same purpose. Eric Mendelsohn's wife recalls their time on the Baltic beaches of Prussia, where he sketched sand dunes: "Eric was deeply impressed by these shapes, and as he drew he would exaggerate or make slight changes to emphasize their architectural qualities" (King 1969, 26). These drawings, which he referred to as "dune architecture" (Figure 5.11), capture both the dunes' windswept forms and his imaginative reactions to them. It is as if the intent is not so much to depict the dunes, but rather to quickly externalize what they stimulate in his mind.

As Mendelsohn drew dunes, Aalto captured northern and Mediterranean landscapes, trees, the patterns of a stone floor,

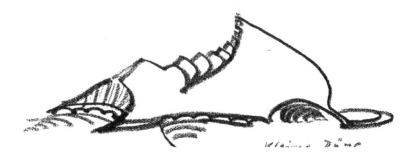

Figure 5.11 Eric Mendelsohn: Small dune, 1920. Perspective. Pencil on paper, 2⅛″ × 6⅛″.

the view from an airplane, and an erupting volcano in his sketchbooks in order to contemplate their patterns through drawing. A most unusual entry is that of a wave in a hurricane (Figure 5.12), remarkable both for its subject matter and for its elaborate and highly articulated development. It is as if the author was fascinated by the crashing waves and endeavored to freeze their form for future reflection. There is a kind of unsettling frenzy in the drawing, but so enigmatic are the shapes and patterns that a viewer might guess the drawing to be of twisted branches blown in the wind.

In making a referential drawing, an author refers to a scene through drawing. But a drawing also refers to its author, offering evidence of his or her intentions. The architect may also refer back to a drawing for information, confirmation, and as stimulus for memories of a prior experience, as when Le Corbusier so frequently turned to his referential sketches from years past as a way to refresh his eye and to recall forms which were relevant to the task at hand. We have also noticed that when we look at our own referential sketches (Figures 5.13 and 5.14), we are vividly reminded of the specifics of the experience, of a windy day with rapidly moving clouds, of the sounds

Figure 5.12 Alvar Aalto: Hurricane, Cape Cod, Massachusetts, 1946. Perspective.

Figure 5.13 Rod Henmi: National
Museum of Western Art, Tokyo, 1992.
Perspective. Ink on paper, 11″ × 8½″.

and smells of a place, of the quality of light brushing the side of
a building, of the sandy texture of stone, of the moist, cool
feeling of being inside. Turning to a sketchbook is to invoke
memories, catalyzing an outpouring of detailed impressions. It
is this aspect of a representation that has made the referential
sketch a valued tool for insight and inspiration. When one
studies another person's travel sketches, they help reveal that
person's way of looking at the objects they depict. And when
one refers to one's own drawings, the abstractions involved in
the drawing process help to reveal and reaffirm particular
concerns, thus not only recalling, but reinforcing a particular
way of seeing.

Figure 5.14 Iain Fraser: Tomb at Bellefontaine Cemetary, St. Louis, Missouri, 1989. Perspective. Ink on paper, 6″ × 9″.

Chapter 6

Diagrams

Diagrams are those drawings which engage in a self-conscious reductive process, attempting to make clear a specific interpretation through the exclusion of that information which the authors deem irrelevant. Yet the differences between diagrams and conventional orthographic, axonometric, or perspectival drawings are subtle and relative, making it difficult to establish a clear boundary. This relativity is illustrated by a series of eighteen axonometric drawings by Peter Eisenman of House IV (Figure 6.1). In subtly differentiated stages, the drawings indicate a rigorous transformational process based on a set of

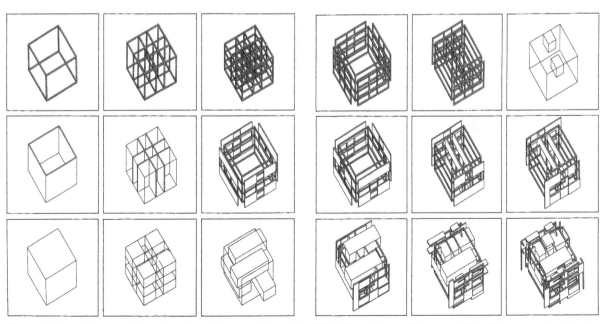

Figure 6.1 Peter Eisenman: Transformational diagrams, House IV, 1971. Plan obliques. (Courtesy of Peter Eisenmann, Architect).

predetermined rules. They show a sequence that moves both from top to bottom and from left to right. The top row depicts manipulations involving the frame, the second planar changes, the third volumetric transformations. As the drawings move from left to right, the articulation of space and mass increases. The "end" result may be seen in the last drawing in the lower right-hand corner, which gives the final configurations of walls, frame, and volumes.

In this sequence of drawings, is a diagram of the project found in the first or third or fifth column of drawings? How much does the information of a project need to be reduced in order to be defined as a diagram? Is there a point at which the act of elimination is too much, sacrificing important aspects so that the diagram becomes misleading, incorrect, or incomplete? In this set of gradually changing forms, each drawing to the left of another could be called a diagram of the other. Yet even the last drawing is still diagrammatic in the sense that it does not delineate many details such as window and door frames, roof edges, material changes, etc. This final drawing could still be considered a diagram when compared to a highly refined axonometric such as the drawings of the Electra Bookstore by Stirling in Chapter 3 (see Figure 3.4).

This set of drawings demonstrate that every drawing is an abstraction, where authors make choices of what and how to draw: a line for an edge; tone as a shaded plane; a scrawled pattern as texture. Each of these choices involve a process of elimination and reduction, subduing certain aspects while highlighting others. The advantage of diagrams is their ability to simplify the consideration of formal or conceptual qualities by minimizing the elements presented. Their essence is analysis. By isolating specific aspects of a subject, a diagram allows one to clarify other features and compare one subject with another or the same subject seen through different filters.[1] The possibilities of graphic codification limit the interpretive result, but the similarity of graphic format allows one to easily see two or more things in an equivalent way. Diagrams aim for clarity and conciseness, avoiding ambiguity and focusing on one specific issue in isolation. By establishing a consistent graphic filter, diagrams are effective tools to compare different situations. Discovering the common elements shared by buildings, spaces, or cities, diagrams give visual form to a specific issue or aspect. In a sense, they can generalize about seemingly disparate things, rhetorically presenting their specific interpretations and conclusions.

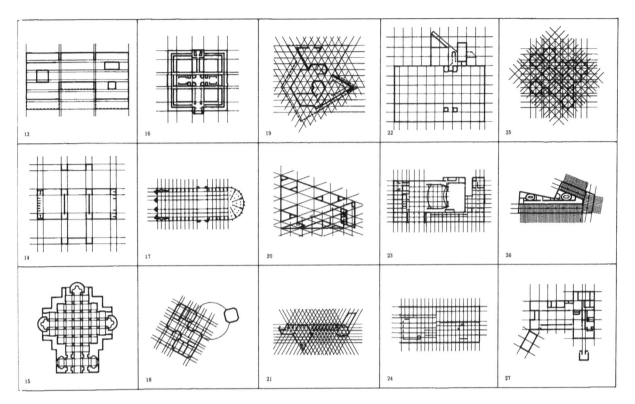

Roger Clark and Michael Pause aptly demonstrate this point in their book *Precedents of Architecture*, which was developed to compare the formal properties of noted buildings. In Figure 6.2, fifteen plan diagrams compare the effects of regulating grids on building composition. Collectively, they reveal a great variety of configurations that regulating grids may take, the role they play in the coordination of the designs, and the commonalities of geometric order in buildings which vary greatly in size, purpose, construction, and historical period. In each diagram, thin regulating lines of plaid, triangulated, shifted, or rotated grids appear as a background upon which the abstracted footprint of the building's plan is superimposed in thicker, bolder lines. The drawings depict regularities of pattern, rhythm, proportion, and geometry as well as variations, irregularities, exceptions, and the addition or insertion of unique and nonconforming elements.

The office of Richard Meier and Partners uses diagrams to serve a series of functions, including designing and presenting. They use diagrammatic sketches in the office as they design, helping to reinforce conceptual concerns and clarifying the development of the design to themselves. They also use diagrams to elucidate their formal and conceptual intentions to an outside audience. An example of the latter are five diagrams for their project for the Royal Dutch Paper Mills Headquarters Building

Figure 6.2 Roger Clark and Michael Pause: Comparative plan diagrams (published in *Precedents in Architecture, 1985*).

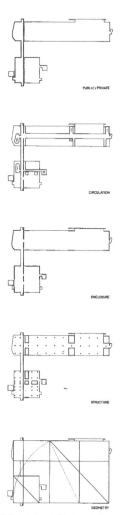

Figure 6.3 Richard Meier & Partners, Architects: Royal Dutch Paper Mills Headquarters, Hilversum, Netherlands, 1987–92. Plan diagrams.

in Hilversum, the Netherlands (Figure 6.3). Comparing each of the drawings to the first level plan (Figure 6.4) illustrates the ability of diagrams to reduce information of some types in order to increase clarity in other ways. For example, the diagram of structure eliminates all indications of partition walls, stairs, openings between floors, bathroom fixtures, etc. The drawing has stripped the plan to essential structural features, indicating at a glance one of the ordering principles of the building. In a similar manner, the circulation diagram clarifies the idea of two primary perpendicular linear corridors intersected by shorter cross corridors by simplifying their actual plan shapes. By eliminating many details such as recessed doorways and depicting the corridor with straight sides, the diagram clarifies the role of the space to be a linear connector. In the public/private diagram, the linear solid wall indicated in all of the diagrams can be seen as a formal element delineating the difference between functional zones. Here the drawing connects the role of a formal element to a conceptual ordering principle.

As illustrations of a singular issue, of geometry, public/private, structure, circulation, or enclosure, each diagram forces a viewer to see a particular aspect, to focus on a particular issue, in a sense to see the intentions of a plan. An author eliminates from a diagram all that he or she considers extraneous to its particular focus, showing a concentrated interpretation by extracting everything else. In these diagrams, eliminating information from the plan drawing helps clarify how this building has been ordered on a proportional system, how an important long stone wall acts as a conceptual divider between public and private, how structure articulates the circulation

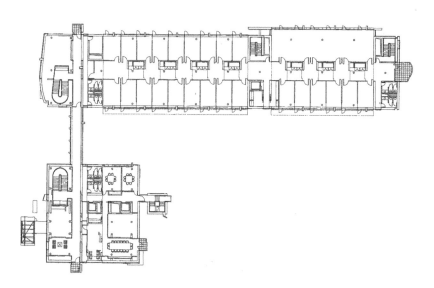

Figure 6.4 Richard Meier & Partners, Architects: Royal Dutch Paper Mills Headquarters, Hilversum, Netherlands, 1987–92. First Level Plan.

system and vice versa, how enclosure highlights particularly important spaces. Each of these diagrams is a wordless explanation, a mode of clarification.

In the Museum for the Decorative Arts in Frankfurt am Main, Germany, Meier illustrates the formal ordering systems of the building through plan and elevation diagrams. The five analytical diagrams (Figure 6.5) clarify the seemingly complex geometry laid out in the two plans by indicating the geometric order of the formal beginning points. In sequence, the set moves from the plan of the existing villa, to the villa inscribed in a sixteen-square grid, to a second grid shifted parallel and perpendicular to the alignment of the river, to a vertical line which relates to the site context, and finally to a new courtyard space, a void equivalent in volume to the existing villa. Having viewed the diagrams, the plans can now be more clearly seen as organized around sixteen squares with three of the four corner squares defined by the gallery spaces of the new part and the fourth by the existing villa. The diagrams make clear that the three corner gallery spaces reiterate the original villa in both size and placement. In addition, the oblique line of the skylit main circulation system can be seen as geometry derived from the alignment of the river. In other words, the diagrams show more clearly how the new construction is intended to make a conceptual linkage to the existing villa and river through the formal ordering systems.

Any drawing type whether orthographic, axonometric, or perspectival, can be used for diagrams. In an example of a use of an elevation for diagrammatic purposes, Meier uses four drawings (Figure 6.6) to formally link the facades of the original villa to the new building. The grid that overlays the facade of the original villa does not always correspond precisely to window openings and patterns, but the drawing demonstrates clearly the degree of correspondence and the discrepancies. Secondly, the viewer is left with the image of the gridded facades of both old and new, in effect seeing the two as tied together by a common regulating order. The diagram leaves its impression, highlighting the architect's intention.

When an architect needs to clarify or summarize a design or some important aspect of it in a quick, synoptic manner, he or she sometimes produces a "thumbnail" diagram sketch. By compressing a scheme into a compact format, as small as an inch or two, a "thumbnail" drawing presents a simplified,

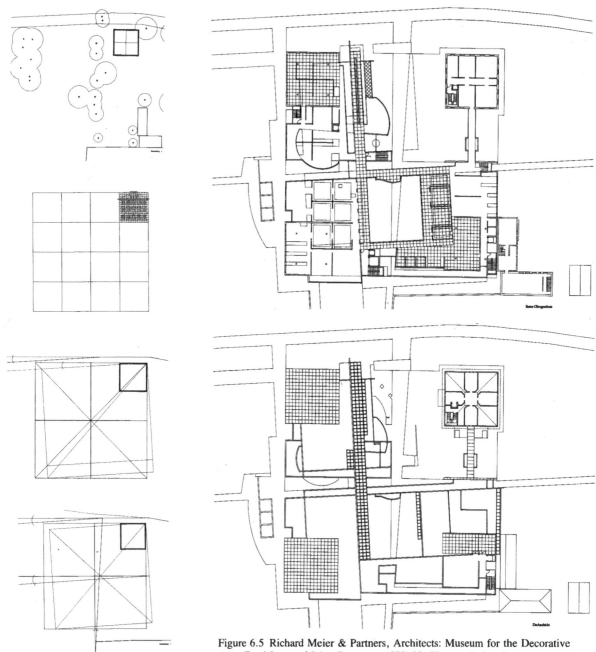

Figure 6.5 Richard Meier & Partners, Architects: Museum for the Decorative Arts, Frankfurt am Main, Germany, 1979–85. Plans and plan diagrams.

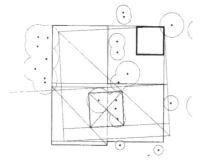

abstracted, and therefore diagrammatic version of a design. Its small size makes drawing details difficult, requiring each mark to be thoughtfully considered and significant. Because of the small format, each line becomes relatively large in proportion to the white space of the paper, increasing its individual impact and presence. An example is Figure 6.7, a series of sketch diagrams by Helmut Jahn of Murphy/Jahn for the State of

Illinois Building in Chicago, Illinois. The illustration is of two small sheets drawn one week apart, each only 5½-by-4¼ inches. In the series of drawings on the right, Jahn indicates eight different schemes through small plans and axonometrics. Each pair of drawings shows a plan and massing strategy, quickly and simply revealing through a consistent graphic format a set of formal and spatial possibilities. He contrasts a "broken donut" shape to a tower on the west or north, a "cut block plaza" to a "curved block." The reduction of buildings to simplified forms allows a comparison of type and scheme by eliminating detail and specific articulation of these shapes.

In the second set of drawings to the left, Jahn uses quick cryptic graphic codes to diagram a treatment for the exterior skin and base. He uses simple abstracted patterns to symbolize treatment of arcaded base and glazed skin, eliminating detail in order to concentrate attention on the idea of the curved shape resting on a heavier base. Finally, a diagram of the site just to the right shows the footprint of the new project in the extreme upper left and indicates in solid black important buildings and their locations. The drawing emphasizes patterns and locations relative to open space, clarifying the relationship of new to existing.

A comparison of Arata Isozaki's visually striking diagram of the Museum of Modern Art, Gunma, Japan (Figure 6.8), to a

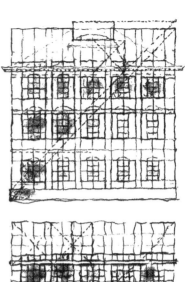
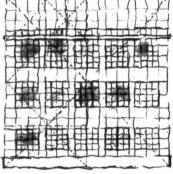

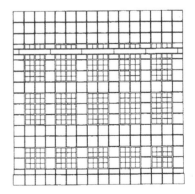

Figure 6.6 Richard Meier & Partners, Architects: Museum for the Decorative Arts, Frankfurt am Main, Germany, 1979–85. Elevational studies.

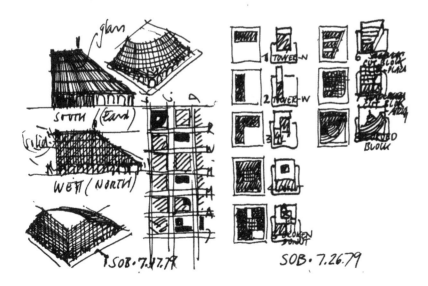

Figure 6.7 Helmut Jahn (Murphy/Jahn): State of Illinois Building, Chicago, Illinois, 1981. Plan and axonometric sketches. Ink on paper, two sheets, 5½″ × 4¼″.

Figure 6.8 Arata Isozaki: Cubic frame study drawing, Museum of Modern Art, Gunma, Japan, 1971. Plan oblique.

Figure 6.9 Arata Isozaki: Museum of Modern Art, Gunma, Japan, 1971. Photograph by Yasuhiro Ishimoto.

photograph of the built museum (Figure 6.9) demonstrates the capabilities of a diagram to remove elements and concretize a particular and sometimes obscure interpretation. The diagram indicates his interpretation of the building as a set of cubic modular frames. He has eliminated any indication of exterior skin, materiality, and interior spatial differentiations. Stark frames cast shadows on the ground, defining an abstracted and altered view of the building. The photograph depicts one view of reality, while the diagram clarifies a reduced but potent other.

Another reality that remains purely conceptual but clearly a force in the figural composition is the ideal of a sphere, diagrammed as a circle in the elevation of Thomas Jefferson's Library at the University of Virginia (Figure 6.10). Though

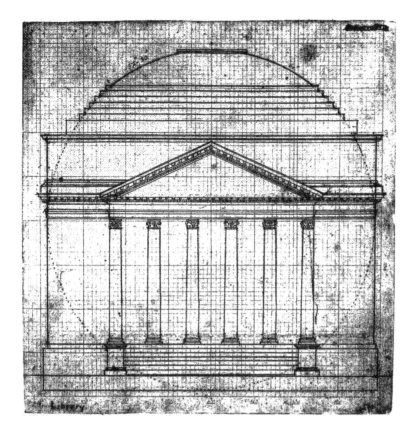

Figure 6.10 Thomas Jefferson: Rotunda, The University of Virginia, Charlottesville, Virginia, c. 1821. Elevation. Ink on gridded paper, 8¾″ × 8¾″ (Thomas Jefferson Papers, Special Collections Department, Manuscripts Division, University of Virginia Library).

represented in the building only by a portion of the roof and completed in the drawing by arcs of carefully spaced dots, it is the essence of the scheme, symbolizing wholeness and perfection and helping to order the geometry of project. Having experienced the diagram, viewers are predisposed to look for the wholeness of the circle/sphere and the idea of perfection both in the design and in the built form. The diagram becomes an icon of the ideal.

In Figure 6.11, Colin Rowe and Fred Koetter use figure/ground diagrams to make a dramatic graphic and conceptual comparison in their book *Collage City*. Two examples of contrasting paradigms for urbanism are presented: one of Le Corbusier's project for Saint-Dié and the other of medieval Parma. The striking drawings by Wayne Copper, where the "figure" or mass of the buildings is indicated in black and the "ground" or void of space is left white, highlight the reversal between the two designs of the proportion and configuration of public space to building mass. The clarity of the differences is a function of greatly reduced data: Information of height and use are eliminated, as are facade treatment, material, transparency, and entry, in addressing the singular issue of the relationship of

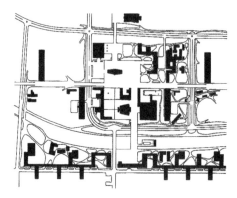

Figure 6.11 Wayne Cooper: Figure/ground drawing of Le Corbusier's plan for the city center, Saint-Dié, France, and of Parma, Italy (published in *Collage City*, 1978). Figure/ground plan diagrams.

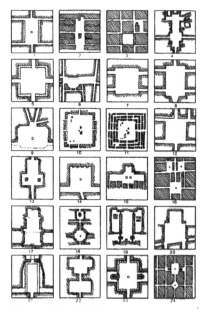

Figure 6.12 Rob Krier: "Orthogonal Plans for Squares," 1975. Plan diagrams.

solid to void. The selection of what to show (building footprint), how to show it (in plan), and what to leave out (height and just about everything else) are critical tactical choices in the debate. The contrast gives dramatic support and visual presence to an ideological point of view.

In a second example of urban diagrams, Rob Krier compares twenty-four different urban spaces (Figure 6.12), emphasizing the manner in which space is defined by buildings. Although these urban squares were constructed at times ranging from 1284 until 1971 and located in cities from Italy to England, the use of the same drawing construct (plan view) and the same graphic technique (line drawing with diagonal line hatching for tone) for each allows one to see them in an equivalent way. Dark hatched tones focus attention on white voids defined by the surrounding dark. What is clearly defined by the graphic technique is urban space (as a resultant void) surrounded and defined by dense building fabric with streets leading into the space. Solid and void, space and containment, figure and ground are brought out unambiguously and exclusively. Omitted from considerations in these drawings are aspects such as paving patterns and materials of the spaces, heights and elevational treatments of surrounding buildings, functional uses of spaces and buildings, sizes, colors, etc. Each of the illustrated squares *could* be graphically described and compared in a variety of other ways, but it is the ability of drawing to exclude information and thereby to highlight specific considerations that allows these spaces to be emphasized as space and to be compared in shape and access. Krier's method presents an edited, abstracted vision of a series of places that enables an equivalent comparison otherwise unperceivable.

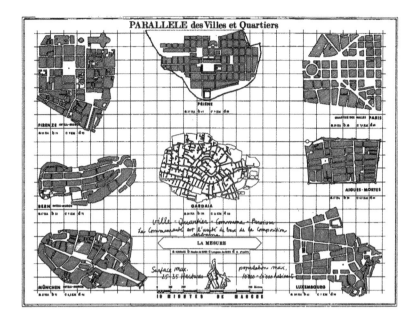

Figure 6.13 Leon Krier: "Parallel of Cities, the Human Dimension," 1978. Plan diagrams.

Leon Krier graphically compares and contrasts seven European cities, relating places of very different character and quality to each other (Figure 6.13). Drawn to the same scale, with the same graphic technique and degree of abstraction, the drawings manifest commonalities of scale in block size and street width, pattern and size of open spaces, and of density of building mass. Representing different traditions and attitudes of city building, they are brought together on the same sheet and compared graphically and statistically. The shape and size of their urban spaces and the patterns and sizes of streets are shown in the common cross-hatching of the blocks. The streets and public spaces are represented by voids of white, while comparative statistical data is provided below each diagram for surface area, the number and length of streets, and the number of blocks. A final distinguishing feature of the drawing is the underlying grid, scaled and proportioned to walking time. Each square represents one hundred meters, eight of which take ten minutes to cross, allowing one to calculate pedestrian travel time. Thus each city is compared graphically by patterns of building masses and streets, quantitatively by cumulative statistics, and experientially by the measure of time.

Walter Gropius diagrammed the relationship of building height to open space in a set of highly abstracted drawings (Figure 6.14) in order to illustrate his ideas about the reordering of high-density dwelling on the hygenic criteria of fresh air, sunshine, and open space. His drawings promote an architecture based on these particular, radical, and quite limited criteria. For example, diagrams *a* (plan) and *b* (section) show

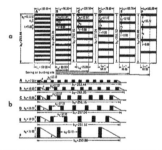

Fig. 40 a, b, c, d: Diagram showing the development of a rectangular site with parallel rows of apartment blocks of different heights. Conditions as to air, sun, view and distance from neighbor block are improved with increased heigth of the blocks in c and d. In a and b these conditions are constant, but the higher the buildings the less land is needed for the same amount of living space.

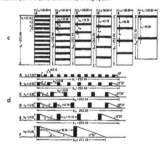

Figure 6.14 Walter Gropius: "Diagram showing the development of a rectangular site with parallel rows of apartment blocks of different heights" (published in *Scope of Total Architecture*, 1937). Plan and section diagrams.

that increased building height reduces the amount of land needed for the same dwelling area. Alternatively *c* and *d* claim to show increased "improvement" in conditions of air, sun, view, and distance from adjacent blocks. The diagrams are filled with quantitative notes on building height and site dimensions, distances between buildings, degrees of sun elevation, and cryptic algebraic notations comparing site dimensions or sun angle increases. The drawings have a particularly rational character, authoritative in their accurate and comparative measurement, but exclude many issues of mass dwelling and urban form, such as human scale, orientation, and access and connection to urban thoroughfares.

The drawing by Louis Kahn of downtown Philadelphia's traffic flow (Figure 6.15) represents an entire type of diagram in which intangible factors such as movement, access, sound, view, function, and time are symbolized and thus given visible form. Buildings and other structures, sidewalks, streetscape, and park landscape have been omitted, highlighting Kahn's particular focus on vehicular issues. Through its density of arrows and dots, the drawing gives the viewer an immediate impression of intensity of use and correspondingly the importance for traffic flow of specific streets. It shows directions of movement, clockwise or counterclockwise, around each block and eddies of flow created by the dominance of one-way streets. Also shown are areas which are effectively vehicle-free (parks and blocks) and those that are densely packed with side streets or alleys.

Every drawing can be considered diagrammatic in the sense that it involves a process of abstraction and a corresponding reduction of information. Each graphic selects parts of the infinite visual data available, interpreting reality through conventionalized or idiosyncratic filters. A plan diagram defines a plan in a particular manner; an axonometric diagram removes elements and therefore adds meaning of a different type. Diagrams offer the capability to take this degree of abstraction beyond the normal conventions of other drawing applications, pushing a level of reduction for rhetorical and analytical reasons. Intrinsically, therefore, diagrams critique and, in their act of reduction, increase understanding.

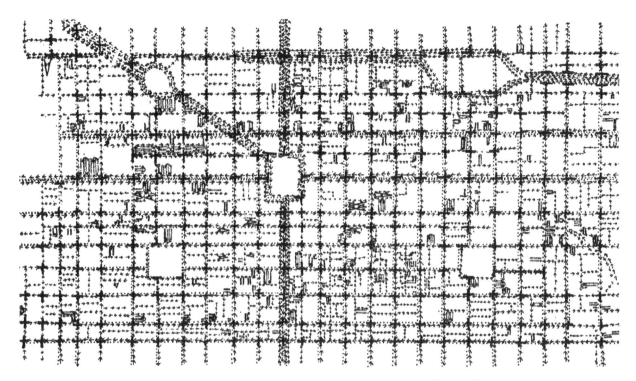

Figure 6.15 Kahn, Louis I.: "Traffic Studies, Center City, Philadelphia." Project, 1952. Plan of existing movement pattern. Ink on white paper, 25¼" × 42". (Collection, The Museum of Modern Art, New York. Gift of the architect).

Chapter 7

Design Drawings

I want to see things. I don't trust anything else. I place things in front of me on the paper so that I can see them. I want to see therefore I draw (the words of Carlo Scarpa, as quoted in Murphy 1990, 12).

Carlo Scarpa used drawing in a manner analogous to his architecture, layering drawing over drawing, compulsively sketching every joint and connection, packing small views of different parts into crevices of a sheet, intertwining them into a rich tapestry of pattern and color like his buildings themselves. He built his drawings like his buildings were built.[1] In a plate studying the tomb at the Brion Cemetery in San Vito d'Altivole, Italy (Figure 7.1), one can see this richly layered, densely packed manner of drawing. At the top of the page he draws a plan, pulls the lines down in order to construct a section, and then uses this drafted base to provide a dimensionally accurate framework for further graphic contemplation and the coordination of studies carried out elsewhere on the sheet.[2] Both plan and section show the results of his graphic layering: Areas of tone and texture have been added; profiles tested by freehand outlines; human figures and plantings drawn in to give a sense of scale and the results over time of vegetation. He uses verbal notes and light, delicate lines to mark moments of brief contemplation. He fills the sheet with different types of drawings to study many different aspects at different scales, such as axonometric sketches which show the roof form and detail sketches which study roof openings and joints. The sheet is filled yet seems to be awaiting the next round of graphic investigation. It remains open-ended, an invitation to continue the graphic conversation and seek out the next level of design evolution.

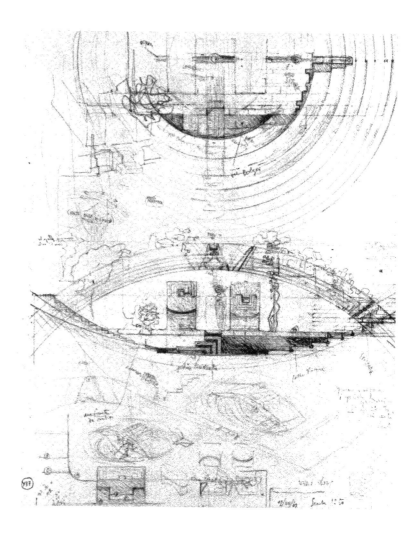

Figure 7.1 Carlo Scarpa: "Plan for the tomb cover," Brion family cemetery, San Vito d'Altivole, Italy, c. 1969. Plan, section, isometric. Pencil and colored pencil on paper, 13⅝″ × 11″.

Design drawings such as Scarpa's are done primarily as a way to study architecture, to find and test ideas, to enter and develop the process of inspiration, invention, and exploration. The first chapter demonstrated in detail the working method of Le Corbusier. Here, the role drawing plays in the designing process of other architects is illustrated, showing the activity of drawing in the development of their architecture. The examples are anecdotal, representing individual approaches. The intent is not to define design drawings through formal characteristics, nor by type, technique, or method, but rather to illustrate different ways that drawing is used for design: freehand and gestural, hardline and precise, thumbnail or large, quickly and roughly, or slowly and carefully. They do not look the same. Rather than a formal similarity, the characteristics they share are within the minds of their makers. Intended as means for private discovery, design drawings are often less self-conscious about graphic conventions and "correctness." What is correct is whatever works for the author.

Different phases have been defined for design drawings. These are usually: first, rough, small sketches, referred to as initial, first, or conceptual drawings; second, larger, scaled freehand and hardline developmental drawings; and third, hardlined, precise definitive drawings.[3] Although this taxonomy appears to be generally valid, the choice was made here not to employ these breakdowns. Different architects' working methods vary so much that it is likely in some situations a definitive drawing for one serves as an initial sketch for another. Architects approach design drawing in a variety of ways, some in a seemingly rigorous linear process of increasing definition and precision, while others seem to move back and forth from gesture to hardline, from small to large.

Scarpa, for example, treats the whole plate as a design endeavor, refining the drawing and design with literally dozens of small studies of details, joints, profiles, and patterns in plan, section, elevation, or perspective. Despite the intensity of graphic study, his densely packed sheets of drawings seldom seem to definitively fix the projects. In his elevation and section of the chapel at Brion (Figure 7.2), he casts shadows, adds color, tone and texture, and embellishes the drawing with figures and vegetation, creating a sense of the character and mood of the place. Yet even this most carefully polished part of the study seems simply a means to focus on further elaboration. By the time he finished the sheet, the more precise drawings of

Figure 7.2 Carlo Scarpa: "Elevation and section of the chapel," Brion family cemetery, San Vito d'Altivole, Italy, c. 1969. Pencil and crayon on cartridge paper, 17½" × 39".

elevation and section were not necessarily the most important; rather, they served as critical devices for identifying conditions requiring further study and investigation, a kind of graphic framework of accurate measure on which to base and coordinate further development.

Each drawing for Scarpa is a carefully crafted construction wherein layers of information are coordinated by thoughtful investigation and correlation. Scarpa's penchant for drawing over another drawing as idea is connected to idea is shown in this sheet (Figure 7.3) for the design of the candelabra of the Brion chapel. Here longitudinal and transverse section cuts are rotated about each other and within elevations, producing a graphic amalgamation of intertwined complexity. It is impossible for the viewer to be certain what part belongs to which view and vice versa. Even the surrounding drawings bleed together. This is not just many related but separate views crowded onto the same sheet. It is virtually a series of drawings made into a single composition, the result of a complex building up of precise marks, both measured and freehand, linked by projected views and inspiration.

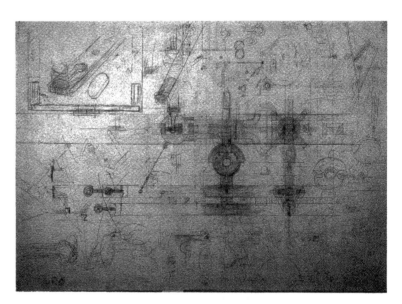

Figure 7.3 Carlo Scarpa: "Study for detailing of the candelabrum," Brion family cemetery, San Vito d'Altivole, Italy, c. 1969. Pencil and crayons on Bristol board.

For Louis Kahn, drawing was a method of gradual evolution and discovery. As described by one of his colleagues, he used vine charcoal on yellow trace, marking and erasing, dynamically thinking on paper (Meyers 1987, xxv). In Figure 7.4, a floor plan sketch of an early scheme for the Kimbell Art Museum in Fort Worth, Texas, Kahn layers broad strokes of charcoal, drawing and removing walls, closing and opening space, shifting rooms and functions, leaving light traces of

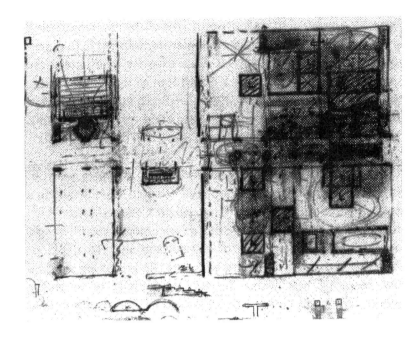

Figure 7.4 Louis I. Kahn: Kimbell Art Museum, Fort Worth, Texas, 1968–69. Plan and sections. Charcoal on yellow trace, 24″ × 30″. (Copyright 1977 Louis I. Kahn Collection, University of Pennsylvania and Pennsylvania Historical and Museum Commission.)

charcoal which gradually build up on the sheet to create an emerging form. The medium of charcoal on trace is well suited for this type of design activity for it is easily manipulated, tugged and pulled, scraped and redrawn like a palimpsest. This sketch also indicates another habit, his use of arrows and circular shapes to help concentrate his attention on experiential qualities of entry, movement, and space. Finally, when Kahn reaches a point of resolution, he uses spray fixative to seal and set the conclusion.

In an elevation study of the Salk Institute for Biological Studies, La Jolla, California (Figure 7.5), Kahn uses tone to bring out the three-dimensionality of the scheme, laying down a rich and rapid tonal background of trees to bring out the white of the buildings and define the space between the two sets of labs. Again, the drawing demonstrates areas of changes, such as an erased area to the far right. Patterns on the elevation have also

Figure 7.5 Louis I. Kahn: Salk Institute Laboratories, La Jolla, California, 1960–61. Elevation. Charcoal on yellow trace, 20″ × 91″. (Copyright 1977 Louis I. Kahn Collection, University of Pennsylvania and Pennsylvania Historical and Museum Commission.)

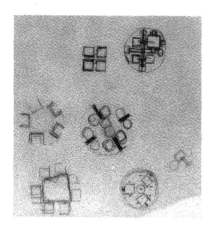

Figure 7.6 Louis I. Kahn: Salk Institute Laboratories, La Jolla, California, 1960–61. Plan studies. Graphite on yellow trace, 14½″ × 18″. (Copyright 1977 Louis I. Kahn Collection, University of Pennsylvania and Pennsylvania Historical and Museum Commission.)

been tried and altered. In retrospect, one of the more interesting propositions is the four lines of poplar trees drawn in the inner space, which represents a test of an idea for landscaping the central space. This drawing allowed him to set the idea in his mind and to consider it; eventually he did change the landscaping scheme considerably, leaving the plaza empty of all plantings and articulated only by paving and a thin channel of water.

Kahn drew for wide ranging reasons, from comparative conceptual diagrams to the development of small scale detail. In a study for the Salk Institute Conference Center (Figure 7.6), Kahn draws a series of alternative arrangements, establishing a quick display for purposes of comparison and visualization. Running through a repertoire of forms, he is making a visual list, inspiring new forms through the activity of recording others. For more detailed development of Salk Laboratories, Kahn tests the arrangements of fins and openings from the offices toward the ocean in a sequence of plan studies (Figure 7.7). The drawing is distinctive in the way that it presents the angled walls in isolation, eliminating the context of the rest of the building. As a result, the drawing is more abstract, with its series of diagonal charcoal lines resembling a musical score. Like a diagram, the drawing reduces information and focuses Kahn's eye on a specific element.[4] In a drawing showing much more refined development of the same condition (Figure 7.8), Kahn sketches the plan refinements in great detail and with considerable control. His notes include instructions to his office, philosophical ideas about the relationship between concrete and wood, and detailed requirements, including di-

Figure 7.7 Louis I. Kahn: Salk Institute Laboratories, La Jolla, California, 1960–61. Plan, wall detail studies. Charcoal on yellow trace, 15″ × 31″. (Copyright 1977 Louis I. Kahn Collection, University of Pennsylvania and Pennsylvania Historical and Museum Commission.)

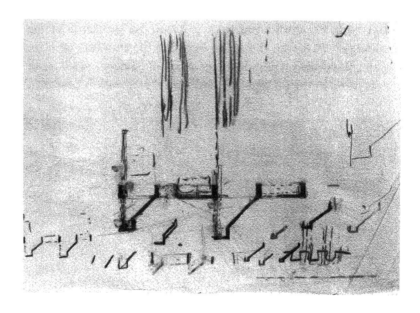

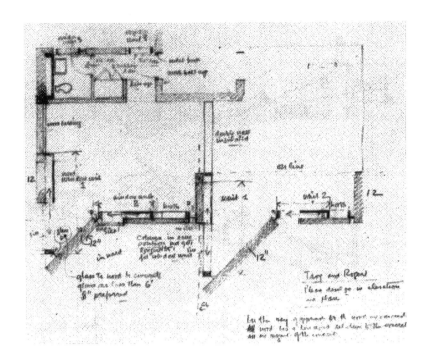

Figure 7.8 Louis I. Kahn: Salk Institute Laboratories, La Jolla, California, 1960–61. Plan. Graphite on yellow trace, 12″ × 16¾″. (Copyright 1977 Louis I. Kahn Collection, University of Pennsylvania and Pennsylvania Historical and Museum Commission.)

mensions for glass. The drawing here is an instrument of detailed execution and large-scale study, not one of changing ruminations like the plan study of the Kimbell Art Museum.

Mario Corea enters enthusiastically into drawing as a means of expression and exploration for his designs. He continually emphasizes the importance of drawing as a means of visualization, analysis, and speculation. His drawings embody the pleasures of both designing and drawing. Three sheets represent his design for an enclosed swimming pool in Badalona, Spain: two made as the design developed, and one drawn after the design was completed. The three drawings represent three different aspects of the design considered through three different drawing formats, plan, axonometric, and perspective, testing such diverse issues as arrangement, form, view, and detail composition. The first sheet (Figure 7.9) contains three freehand ink sketches: at the top a site plan sketch which shows the end spaces emphasized and articulated as figural wholes, while the pool enclosure in the middle remains undeveloped; at the bottom, a perspective view looks through the arched gate of the enclosing wall into the entry court; and in the middle, a small, quick axonometric sketch configures the form and the front of the pool building. The second sheet (Figure 7.10) contains two long, low perspective sketches, which represent the project from opposing views. They exaggerate proportions, stretching length in a graphic statement of architectural intention. The striking energy of these drawings is conveyed by

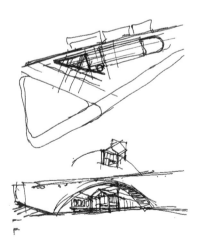

Figure 7.9 Mario Corea: Covered swimming pool, Badalona, Spain. Plan, axonometric, perspective sketch.

119

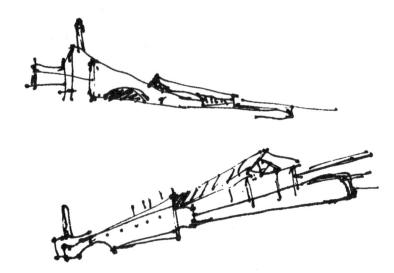

Figure 7.10 Mario Corea: Covered swimming pool, Badalona, Spain. Perspective sketches.

quick, bold ink line strokes, drawn so vigorously, they sometimes overlap intersections with other lines or stop short. The counterposition of views from each end of the building show at once the contrast of experience and their linkage through the shared view of the wall with its gate. Combined, the two sketches illustrate the importance of this common element, while the sheet itself represents a much more developed state of the project.

Corea executed the third plate (Figure 7.11) after completing his design in order to reinterpret the finished project through drawing, re-presenting it and thus re-designing it in the sketch. It is a type of referential drawing wherein he draws his own architecture, allowing him to reconsider its forms. This corner view, composed on a faintly drafted outline and rendered freehand in ink and wash, shows the completed building set against a darkly toned sky and atop the foreground wall. Care has been taken to represent details of the construction method, such as concrete tie holes, masonry coursing, vertical striations of the enclosure above the masonry, and the mesh grid of the deck fence. A sense of atmosphere and experiential qualities of the site are rendered by sunlight which casts strong black shadows so that the building appears bright and luminous against a darkly powerful sky. The possibilities of the emerging design in the preconstruction design drawings and of its realized form are reflected in this post-design referential/design drawing.

Alvaro Siza visited St. Louis, Missouri, and spent an afternoon observing and drawing architecture with a group of students.

Figure 7.11 Mario Corea: Covered
swimming pool, Badalona, Spain.
Perspective.

On a cloudy fall day, he and the students surreptitiously pried
open a chain link gate and slipped into the curving vertical space
of a vacant industrial building. Everyone drew, Siza with quiet
intensity, rapidly marking ink lines. Wherever they went that
day, he drew, standing slightly away from the group, bent over
his sketchbook, recording every place he saw. This devotion to
referential sketching is an important part of Siza's design
attitude:

No drawings give me as much pleasure as these:
travel sketches . . .

Figure 7.12 Alvaro Siza: "Rayon in L.C. mother's house," 1981. Perspective sketch.

Suddenly the pencil or Bic begins to fix images, faces in the foreground, faded profiles or luminous details, the hands which draw them. Lines, at first timid, rigid, lacking precision, later obstinately analytical, at moments vertiginously definitive, free until drunkeness; later tired and gradually irrelevant.

In the space of an authentic journey, the eyes, and by means of them, the mind, gain unexpected capacities.

We perceive in a non-mediated way. That which we learned reappears dissolved amongst the lines which we later draw (Siza 1988, 15).

Figure 7.13 Alvaro Siza: "New Goa," 1985. Perspective sketch.

Siza's travel sketches are design sketches in the sense that they are a means to key his vision and to wander through extant architecture. While he draws the forms he is observing, he is also contemplating the designs within his imagination. His lyrical lines seem to dance through a scene, touching, floating, then touching again. Siza often literally places himself in the drawing, his hands reaching out from the page, a cigarette between fingers, a continual reminder of his presence, his figure in the scene. He is at once drawer and drawn, author and subject of the drawing.[5] In his drawings of Le Corbusier's mother's house (Figure 7.12) and of Nova Goa (Figure 7.13), his pen touches surfaces, remakes profiles, and acts as a means to refer to his architecture.

Figure 7.14 Alvaro Siza: Teachers' Training College, Setubal, Portugal, circa 1986. Perspectives.

In his sketches for the design of the Teacher's Training College in Setúbal, Portugal (Figure 7.14), Alvaro Siza looks through the filter of his travel sketches at the space of a project. The human figure is located, studying the scene from a distance in the upper drawing, or moving closer within the enclosing wings of the project. Siza uses the same lilting lines, defines the same intense sense of standing within the space as he does in his referential drawings, in a sense, recreating this technique in the design sketch. His drawing of a commission and his drawing of a travel scene could be interchangeable. They seem to demonstrate not only the same way of drawing but also the same way of looking.

In a composite drawing for the Banco Pinto & Sottomayor in Oliveira de Azemeis, Portugal (Figure 7.15), Siza moves himself into the graphic, drawing both his view as well as the conceptualized representation of that which he is viewing. He uses a crisp hardline plan to depict his intuitive geometric response to site and program. In contrast to the abstractions of a dense pattern of lines in plan, small freehand pencil perspectives on the margins vividly depict the experience of viewing the project from different places. An especially compelling drawing is the one just above the lower left corner that depicts a powerful taut sense of the sweeping curve. Just above that drawing is a faint interior perspective giving a sense of the space. Other drawings show interior and exterior details, helping focus his explorations from whole to part.

Figure 7.15 Alvaro Siza: Banco Pinto & Sottomayor, Oliveira de Azeméis, 1971–74.

Antoine Predock uses drawing in a dynamic, nonlinear, and spontaneous working manner, sketching intensely as a means to discover and depict his ideas. He employs a variety of sketching media, including pen, brush, markers, and pastels, and he uses them in a very tactile, involved way. He demonstrates his use of drawing as an exploratory medium in a series of drawings for the design of the American Heritage Center and Art Museum at the University of Wyoming, Laramie, Wyoming. In a sheet from his sketchbook of some of the first visual and verbal notes for the project (Figure 7.16), Predock cyptically summarizes important ideas for the eventual development of the project, and studies the project through uninhibited flowing lines. The drawings are freehand and only minimally concerned with

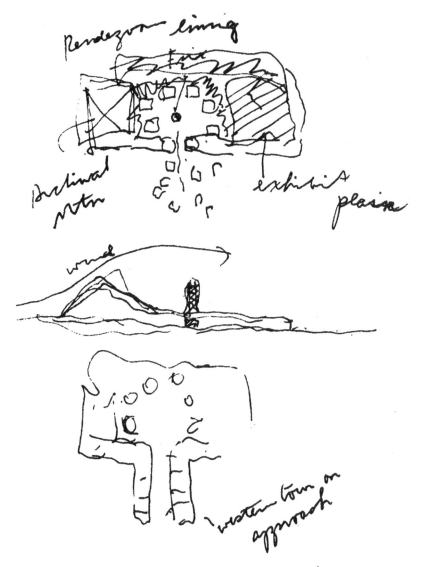

Figure 7.16 Antoine Predock: American Heritage Center and Art Museum, University of Wyoming, Laramie, Wyoming, 1986. Plans, section.

scale, measurement, or precision. In plan, he draws an "archival mountain," rapidly "x-ed" to give it a sense of volume and importance, a centralized "rendezvous" space designating the archetypal Western town, and an "exhibit plain" on the far right. There is an implied orthogonal order but few graphic indications of a rigorous geometric system. The plan at the bottom extracts a portion of the larger plan above and studies it in a larger format, a concentration on the development of an idea for a particular part, removed from its context. Despite the modest level of development at this very early stage in the project, Predock uses the section/elevation to test four different profiles for the "archival mountain." In a process of reiteration he shifts, adjusts, and begins the study of exactly what shape should occur in what way.

In a much larger drawing done on butcher paper (Figure 7.17), Predock wanders through the project with a series of different drawing types and scales, including sections, elevations, plans, site plan, a distant site elevation, and conceptual diagrams. Using the sheet as a widespread repository for his musings, Predock works through each small speculative sketch, including in the lower left corner a section showing a spiraling space which leads to an opening at the top of the "mountain." A tiny site elevation at the bottom center suggests profiles from a

Figure 7.17 Antoine Predock: American Heritage Center and Art Museum, University of Wyoming, Laramie, Wyoming, 1986. Plans, sections, evaluations.

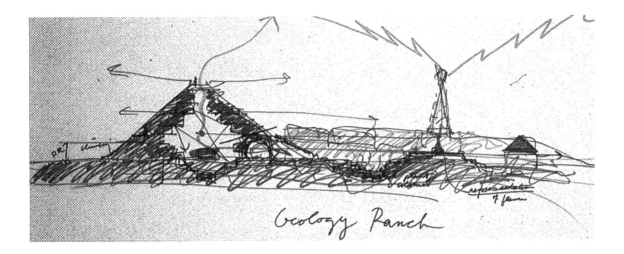

distance. On the far middle right a site plan relates the structure to the campus. Finally in the upper middle portion a plan develops the scheme.

Figure 7.18 Antoine Predock: American Heritage Center and Art Museum, University of Wyoming, Laramie, Wyoming, 1986. Section.

Predock's relaxed manner of drawing at this preliminary stage is exemplified in this section drawing (Figure 7.18), where he uses colored marker and ink lines with playful exuberance, creating an expressive composition with rapidly scrawled lines, arrows, and color and indicates staggered floors which follow the shape of the exterior. This angled profile is reinforced by a reciprocal cut into the base below grade so that the space both climbs and descends. To the right of the "archival mountain," the drawing shows the way the grade has been dug out in a continuation of the "mountain's" contour, as if to wedge a shape into the earth.

In a freehand isometric drawing (Figure 7.19), Predock combines a study of interior structure with an exterior stair leading to the top of the "archival mountain." A rapidly sketched lattice of beams and column is intricately interwoven into a central mast surrounding a chimney. In the lower portion of the page, the interior grid of beams and columns is illustrated, surmounted by a staircase and viewing platform that occurs on the exterior of the mass. The combination of these two produce a simultaneous viewing and a sense of their formal relationship. To the upper right, Predock has also sketched a detail of the connection between chimney mast and lattice, moving from small to large scale and changing drawing type.

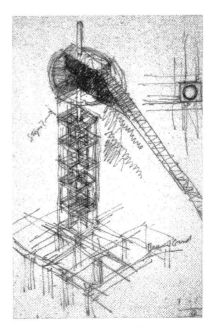

Figure 7.19 Antoine Predock: American Heritage Center and Art Museum, University of Wyoming, Laramie, Wyoming, 1986. Isometric, plans detail.

In a final pair of design drawings, Predock uses bold outlines to define the contours of the primary forms of the project and expressively depict the qualities of their silhouettes. In a

Figure 7.20 Antoine Predock: American
Heritage Center and Art Museum,
University of Wyoming, Laramie,
Wyoming, 1986. Perspective sketch.

colored pastel-and-ink perspective (Figure 7.20), the drawing
places the design proposal in the context of the University of
Wyoming campus. The "archival mountain" and the clustered
village are set into a base of conifers, their shapes linked to the
distant mountains and foreground of indoor and outdoor stadi-
ums. Through a careful, involved tracing of contours, lines of
irregular thickness demarcate form. The pastel medium reinforces these edges, lending drama to the sky. In an even more
reduced, but elegantly simple drawing (Figure 7.21), Predock's
bold, variegated lines trace the outlines and minimally delineate
what he regards as critical to his project. These few lines
interpret the whole, indicating his concerns for the way the
"archival mountain" meets the sky, joins the land, blends into
the contours of the clustered village and conifers, and extends
horizontally. The drawing refers to his own design, a record and
reiteration of a gradual process of exploratory drawing.

In a sense, all drawings are design drawings by virtue of their
contribution directly or indirectly to the architect's task of
imagining, articulating, and refining a design. But the drawings
in this chapter represent several architects' direct attention to a
specific project and the realization of a specific building on a

specific site. They show the remarkable range of issues, values, styles, and points of departure that architects exhibit through their design drawings, and reflect the unique contribution that each individual makes to architecture and its collective legacy.

Figure 7.21 Antoine Predock: American Heritage Center and Art Museum, University of Wyoming, Laramie, Wyoming, 1988. Perspective sketch.

Chapter 8

Presentation Drawings

In the nineteenth century, one of the most influential schools of architecture, the École des Beaux Arts in France, developed elaborate and time-consuming techniques for the preparation of final drawings. In his book describing its methods, *The Study of Architectural Design*, John Harbeson emphasizes the importance of drawings used for presentations. He suggests when setting up a schedule for a twenty-one-day project, one should reserve ten of those days for his or her preparation. In the chapter titled The Psychology of Success, he writes:

A design must be well presented to appeal at once to the jury. This means well drawn and well rendered; the architecture well modelled, the third dimension well expressed; entourage well studied in relation to the architecture and rendered in proper value. It also means that the sheet must be well "composed" . . .

Good drawing and presentation alone . . . will not win a competition—but they always insure a careful consideration on the part of the jury, while a poorly presented drawing is at a great disadvantage in this respect (Harbeson 1926, 291, 297).

This anecdote suggests the importance of and self-consciousness toward the presentation of architectural designs. Architects prepare drawings in order to convince an audience of the merits of a design. In this sense, these **presentation drawings** differ from design drawings, which are prepared as a matter of course during the working process.[1] Presentation graphics require an author to be more conscious of the drawing as a finished product, since they are intended to engage and persuade an outside audience. As a result, these drawings are usually more premeditated and deliberately composed, requiring a greater commitment in time and effort than an equivalent design study.

Presentation drawings constitute a critical and valued segment of the legacy of architectural drawings, as these graphics are usually the most finished, carefully crafted, and "artful" of drawings. They are generally the most public of architectural drawings, as they are often well publicized by the mass media, playing an important role in public understanding before the realization of a project. They establish an image of a building, subsequently influencing the actual experience of walking through the place. For example, the widespread publication of the drawing of Frank Lloyd Wright's Fallingwater (Figure 4.3), has established a preconception in many people's minds which affects their perception when they actually visit the house. In addition, many of these drawings delineate projects that have never been built, constituting the sole means of experiencing and remembering those designs. Finally, these drawings have their own presence, at once related to but independent of the buildings they represent, a lasting impact as a result of their graphic virtuosity.

A design drawing can be enigmatic, laconic, incomplete to an outsider, as the insider/author fills in the missing voids. In contrast, architects aim to make their presentation drawings clear and accessible or consciously choose to portray a particular mood, such as an enigmatic one for a particular reason. These drawings turn their communicative purpose to the outside rather than aiming for clarification by the author to herself or himself. Although many study drawings are precise, measured, and hardline, presentation drawings often show a greater level of detail, development, and specificity. In their preparation, designers must commit to a certain stage of the project; they must stop the intricate dynamics of designing for at least a short time in order to delineate the decisions made up to that point. Presentation drawings are the end results of a graphic process and are thus very different from the open-ended, incomplete character of design drawings.

An example of the incredible elaboration and time involved in the preparation of presentation drawings is this ink wash rendering by Cass Gilbert of the end facade of the Saint Louis Art Museum expansion proposal (Figure 8.1). This drawing demonstrates the style of delineation developed and used at the École des Beaux Arts and propagated in the United States by its graduates, such as Gilbert. The technique of using ink washes requires exacting craftsmanship, wherein one brushes translucent layers of watered ink (as many as twenty or more) to build up values and rich, lush tones.[2] Using this technique, Gilbert

brings out the qualities of a building glowing in sunlight. The plate is three-dimensional, deep, and full, the illusion of depth generated by the careful rendition of cast shadows which are skillfully articulated to create a sense of reflected light in the niches between the columns. A subtle wash is laid over the entire sky area to set off the white of the building. The drawing fixes the building firmly to the ground, using darker tones of plantings and grass to provide a visual base for the composition and to set off the lighter values of stairs, retaining walls, and the building itself.

The difference in attitudes between design and presentation drawings is evidenced by the fact that architectural offices frequently have the latter prepared by professional delineators, freelance individuals who specialize in the business of making compelling, persuasive drawings.[3] In this and the next chapter, two of the drawings of one of the leading professional delineators of the twentieth century, Hugh Ferriss, have been included.

Figure 8.1 Cass Gilbert: "End Pavilion Elevation," Art Museum, Saint Louis, Missouri, 1916. Elevation. Ink and ink wash on paper. (Courtesy of the Saint Louis Art Museum).

Figure 8.2 Hugh Ferriss: "Proposal for Downtown Redevelopment," St. Louis, Missouri, 1945. Perspective. Graphite and ink on trace. (Courtesy of the Missouri Historical Society).

In his drawing of the St. Louis riverfront (Figure 8.2), Ferriss shows his ability to dramatically present architectural proposals, in this case one for the city's riverfront, which was published in a newspaper. He graphically hyperbolizes the project through his manipulation of light and dark, suggestions of motion and reflection, in an effort to capture the imagination and support of the citizenry. Illustrating a bold redevelopment of the riverfront, the aerial night scene looks across the Mississippi from Illinois. The broad panorama depicts a view that an observer would experience if arriving by helicopter. Ferriss's command over tone renders the night scene with rich dark tones accentuated by striking areas of light. The scene glows from certain key nodes and corridors: repetitive facades along a street at the top of the plate, the brightly lit mall, and the luminous interiors of the heliport and of the arriving helicopter. Each glowing point and place celebrates the power of technology to bring night to life, the effect doubled by the reflection of the scene in the river, a vivid and compelling vision of the plan and its progressive theme.

As discussed in Chapter 2 on orthographic drawings, the vertical views of elevations or sections and the horizontal views of a plan need to be cross-referenced or synthesized in the mind in order to understand the three-dimensionality of a project. In a drawing of the Cranbrook School for Boys, Bloomfield Hills, Michigan (Figure 8.3), Eliel Saarinen connects two elevation views and a plan through drawing format and uses pencil technique to create a powerful sense of space, depth, light, and materiality. One can quickly move from the plan upward to the long elevation and easily compare the column in its horizontal and vertical condition. Similarly, one can view the long elevation and "turn the corner" to its short side, shown on the left. Thus the three orthographic views, each presenting two-dimensional information, link themselves and offer an interrelated three-dimensional viewpoint. Saarinen powerfully reinforces this three-dimensionality through his masterful use of the pencil and the conventions of shadow construction. He creates an illusion of depth by carefully crafted chiaroscuro, meticulously building up areas of shade, shadow, and highlight. His graphite strokes run diagonally, reiterating and emphasizing the impression and directionality of the sunlight. He subtly lightens areas with an eraser, creating the impression of glinting reflections. The intense rendition of shade, shadow, and light is so strong that the unrendered portion of the paper becomes a frame for the two elevations.

Figure 8.3 Eliel Saarinen (1873–1950): Elevation and Plan, Proposed Entrance to Art Club, Cranbrook Academy of Art, Bloomfield Hills, Michigan, 1927. Pencil on paper, 24¼″ × 36″. (Collection of Cranbrook Academy of Art Museum, CAAM 1928.37).

In their rendering of the World Financial Center, in New York (Figure 8.4), Cesar Pelli and Associates use a soft pencil technique to reduce building surfaces to smoothly rendered planes in a drawing of abstracted simplicity.[4] Shade and shadow define the volumes, amplifying the sense of crisply modeled masses, while reflections subtly indicate the reflective glazing at the top of the new towers. Light has been cast from the left and drawn in a manner depicting a low, glaring sun that washes out depth and texture. Finally, the project's setting has been powerfully exploited, taking a viewpoint that sets the

Figure 8.4 Cesar Pelli: World Financial Center, New York, New York, 1980–81. Perspective.

project between reflections in water and the sky, adjacent to the twin towers of the World Trade Center. The drawing at once locates the project in context, dramatizes its relationship to water and sky, and complements its forms through graphic technique.

In three orthographic drawings of his Saifukuji Buddhist Temple (Figures 8.5–8.7), Shin Takamatsu demonstrates how a finely grained, highly controlled pencil tone technique brings out depth and texture. He produces an effect of a machined, metallic look in his drawings. Takamatsu refers to his buildings as masks (Takamatsu 1988, 8). For example, in his main elevation of the temple (Figure 8.5), he produces a drawing with a certain brooding and enigmatic character through his handling of deep shadows and suggestion of a hard, smooth material. In his section drawing (Figure 8.6), he creates a spatial entity with a strong sense of three-dimensionality. Again, he casts shadows to increase depth information but in this view the careful grading of tonal values with the darkest tones used for the areas farthest away draws the viewer's attention through the intricate latticework of the temple struc-

Figure 8.5 Shin Takamatsu: Saifukuji Buddhist Temple, Japan, 1982. Elevation.

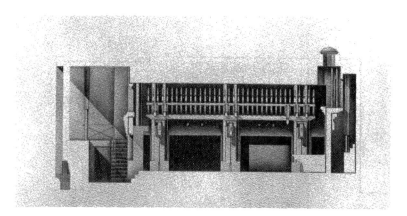

Figure 8.6 Shin Takamatsu: Saifukuji Buddhist Temple, Japan, 1982. Section.

136

ture to the openings beyond. In his plan drawing (Figure 8.7), cast shadows help "pull" the vertical elements of walls and columns away from the page, thereby strongly defining the spatial enclosing elements. The gradation from deep to light tones describes the shadows while the cut walls and columns of the plan have been left white, a reversal of the graphic convention of *poché* in which the plane of dissection cuts open the building and "cut" elements are highlighted with dark tone (or sometimes color). The result is a concentration of value in the interior of the space and a use of lush values on the floor surfaces.

In Figure 8.8, Saarinen, Saarinen and Associates present a serene vision of a starkly elegant artifact, what has come to be known as the St. Louis Arch. The simple composition of the plate emphasizes the two drawings of plan and elevation by

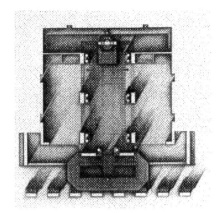

Figure 8.7 Shin Takamatsu: Saifukuji Buddhist Temple, Japan, 1982. Plan.

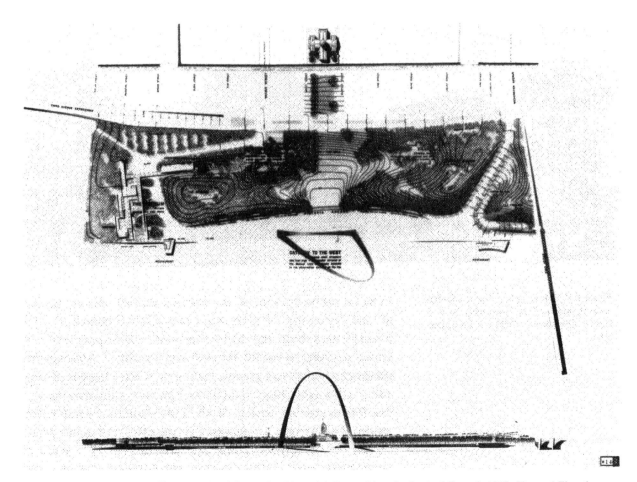

Figure 8.8 Eero Saarinen: Jefferson National Expansion Memorial Competition, St. Louis, Missouri, 1947. Plan and Elevation. Ink, wash, and graphite on paper. (Courtesy of the Jefferson National Expansion Memorial/National Park Service).

careful use of the white space while sections at the bottom were drawn lightly and unobtrusively. The elevation below dramatically renders the arch in dark silhouette against large areas of white space, its soaring form contrasted to the long horizontal defined by trees and ground. Dark tone for the foliage defines an open space leading from the courthouse along with curvilinear drives and walks. Also shown in plan are contour lines indicating the slope of the land. In one of the small sections on the bottom of the plate, the idea for a gradual slope from courthouse to arch to river can be seen on the right. It is interesting to note that despite the beautifully crafted nature of these presentation drawings and their finished appearance, design changes occurred even after their submission. One major change was the location of the arch relative to the axis of the courthouse mall. The drawings show the arch shifted off center of the courthouse. In the eventual construction it was centered.

Figure 8.9 Paul Rudolph: Married student housing project, Yale University, New Haven, Connecticut, 1960–61. Elevation. Ink.

In an elevation drawing of the married student housing project at Yale University, New Haven, Connecticut (Figure 8.9), Paul Rudolph uses shade and shadow and *atmospheric perspective* to create a strong sense of three-dimensionality.[5] Atmospheric perspective refers to a graphic technique where changes in tonal values are used to suggest depth in drawings, similar to the way that foreshortening depicts depth in the traditional perspectival model. This creates a semblance of the effects of depth where distant objects appear lighter and less distinct as a result of atmospheric haze. In this drawing, the impression of precisely modulated and configured masonry layers receding into misty light results from line weights which get thinner as the planes recede in depth, moving the value of tone from robust darkness in the foreground toward whiteness in the back. Only the pattern of the masonry joints remains constant, connecting the layers into a common composition. Glass is rendered by fine diagonal meshes of thicker or thinner lines following the same strategy of darker foreground elements receding to a lighter background. The trees, which also fade into the distance, clarify the overlapping of layered facades.

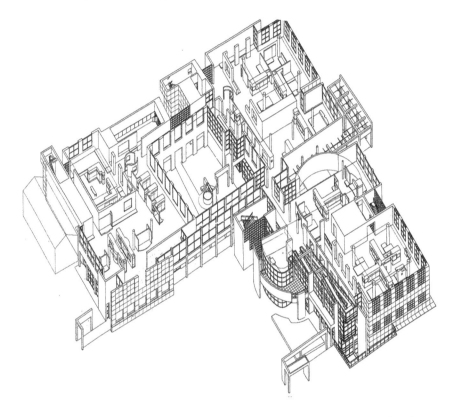

Figure 8.10 Richard Meier & Partners, Architects: Museum for the Decorative Arts, Frankfurt am Main, Germany, 1979–85. Plan oblique.

One of the advantages of axonometric projections is their capability to clearly depict the relationship between interior and exterior spaces. In their drawing for the Museum for the Decorative Arts in Frankfurt am Main, Germany (Figure 8.10; this project is also discussed in Chapter 6), Richard Meier and Partners use the rigor of axonometric drawing to indicate with great specificity the organization and nature of the galleries and supporting rooms while relating these areas to enclosing walls and exterior spaces. One is able to move easily from outside the building, through its envelope, to adjoining interior partitions and furniture. The drawing elucidates horizontal relationships in plan to conditions in the vertical, such as glazing, openings through walls, and the proportions of spaces. Crisp ink lines delineate the placement of elements within the overall building order in a tightly controlled, meticulously precise format.

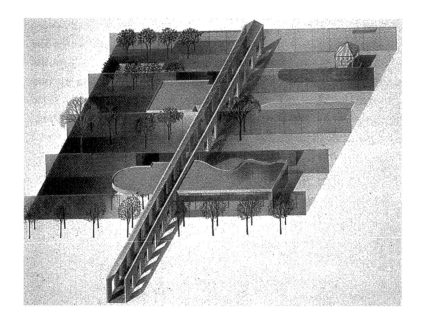

Figure 8.11 Cesar Pelli: Long gallery house proposal for the Venice Biennale, 1977. Elevation oblique.

The drawing by Caesar Pelli and Associates of the single family house proposal for the 1977 Venice Biennale (Figure 8.11) promotes the project's planar and layered conception through its axonometric format while also emphasizing the importance of its material qualities through a meticulously airbrushed full-color technique. The elevation oblique viewpoint reinforces the sense of frontality while the graphic technique of color, tone, and shading renders the reflective and refractive properties of glass and other materials. Throughout the drawing, walls reflect adjacent objects accurately while at the same time allowing objects behind to show through, modeling a domain of unusual indeterminancy and visual change. For example, on the right-hand side of the fourth wall, the pool is reflected on its surface while at the same time the pavilion behind can be seen through the pool's reflection. In another place, the roof of the penetrating portico is rendered reflectively opaque on the left side, and refractively transparent on the right. But perhaps the most mysterious condition of transparency in the project is the seamless, unsupported roof of the freely shaped building in the first yard on the right.

Drawings can both represent specific forms and simultaneously raise questions about representation itself. The use of photomontage, for example, presents a viewer with "the fascinating paradox of being able to distort reality with the medium which was its truest mirror" (Ades 1976, 19). This technique employs photographs of objects, divorces them from their original context, and connects them to new situations, resulting in provocative juxtapositions.[6] The objects depicted bring their

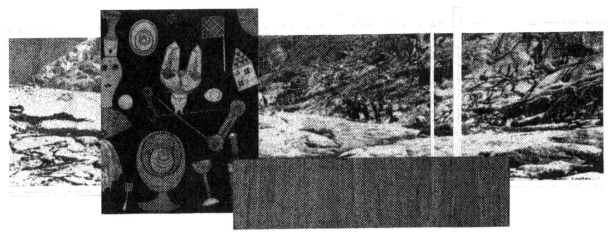

Figure 8.12 Mies van der Rohe, Ludwig: Resor house. Jackson Hole, Wyoming. Project, 1938. Interior perspective of livingroom, looking south. Pencil, wood veneer, cut-out color reproduction (Paul Klee "Bunte Mahlzeit," 1928), and photograph (mountain landscape) on illustration board, 30″ × 40″. (Collection, Mies van der Rohe Archive, The Museum of Modern Art, New York. Gift of the architect).

associations to the new context. In Mies van der Rohe's depiction of the Resor House project in Wyoming (Figure 8.12), he uses photomontage as a graphic rhetorical device to represent his aspiration to relate nature, house, and inhabitants.

The photographs dominate the drawing, inserted between the minimal presence of delicate, precisely drafted lines, which define window mullions, a column, and the edges of ceiling and floor. A photograph of the mountainside represents the view through the glass wall. Placed in front of it are a reproduction of Paul Klee's *Bunte Mahlzeit* and a panel of wood grain. Through his use of photographs, Mies equates a view to the exterior natural world with a work of art and a wall of wood.[7] The view through glass is flattened and compressed, two-dimensional and composed, like the interior space of art and visually rich materials.

Frank Lloyd Wright and his associates used the shapes, proportions and directionality of drawing to influence the perceptual effects. For example, his full-color drawing of the Ward Willitts house (Figure 8.13) uses a horizontal format of almost four to one proportion to reiterate the length and horizontality of the house, creating a condition of sequential viewing from left to right and from right to left, so that the drawing is never quite grasped entirely at once. The perspectival construction reinforces this effect, with a low horizon line and a view at a very slight oblique angle relative to the long side, resulting in little foreshortening of that face and emphasizing its length. In addition, the rhythm of trees produces a segmenting effect, almost dividing the plate into thirds. The ultimate result is of a

Figure 8.13 Frank Lloyd Wright: Ward Willitts house, Highland Park, Illinois, 1902. Perspective. Ink, watercolor, gouache and crayon on paper, 8¾″ × 32½″. (Courtesy of The Frank Lloyd Wright Archives. Copyright © The Frank Lloyd Wright Foundation 1960).

Figure 8.14 Frank Lloyd Wright: Thomas Hardy house, Racine, Wisconsin, 1905. Perspective. Pencil and colored pencil, ink and wash on paper, 19″ × 5½″. (Courtesy of The Frank Lloyd Wright Archives. Copyright © The Frank Lloyd Wright Foundation 1962).

two-dimensional plate which creates a semblance of three-dimensional visual experience in the way that one sees segments, near and far, left and right, then assembles the pieces in the mind. In contrast, in a watercolor perspective of the Thomas Hardy house (Figure 8.14), Wright's office has instead used a vertical format of three to one proportion. This dramatic portrayal of a house set on a bluff at the lake's edge forces the attention of the viewer's gaze to move from water at the base of the plate, past the edge and up along the bank to the house itself, and finally beyond to the sky closing the very top of the drawing. Again the audience sees the view sequentially, an experience that emphasizes the project's relationship to the water.

In her drawing of the Childe Harold Wills house (Figure 8.15), Marion Mahony's distinctive plate composition utilizes a large blank area as an important element in the viewing of the sheet and the project.[8] She leaves more than half of the plate white, pushing three perspectival views to the top of the plate. One has a multiple experience of the building through the views of these three perspectives but also a strikingly singular impression in which each is bound together by the dramatically blackened sky contrasted against the powerful white base. The strength of the white void becoming foreground ties the views into a moment of simultaneity. The center drawing is a distant, frontal, and overall view which distances the viewer as if one were seeing the house while passing in the street. The flanking views are close-ups of front and rear access, the right view moving the viewer up the driveway to the front door, the left moving around the house to the back and positioning the viewer in the garden. Thus, within these drawings, she presents the house in its overall frontality, then rotates it and closes in on it, illustrating the procession of arrival from the street to the front door and then beyond through the arch to the backyard and the pool area.

Drawings can also depict a sequence of vision and the effects of approaching, entering, and moving through a project. In two plates from their winning entry for the Women in Military Service for America Memorial (Figure 8.16), Marion Weiss and Michael A. Manfredi of Weiss/Manfredi Architects use a series of sketches on the left and right edges to indicate the sequence of experience while tying these vignettes to the overall organization of the scheme through drawings in the center and base of each plate. The first plate focuses on the experience of the exterior, using six sketches to show views of approaching from different distances and sights from different points of the outside. The sketches of the second plate depict the interior spaces, including main entry, conference hall, and passages, creating a sense of movement and occupancy. At the same time, all twelve sketches are related to the building as a whole through their juxtaposition with section, plan, and aerial perspective views.

Separate drawing constructions can also be knit together, creating a new drawing type, the combination of varying viewpoints. In a clever combination of plan oblique views of the State of Illinois Building in Chicago, Helmut Jahn of Murphy/Jahn interlocks a down view with an up view (Figure 8.17). The down view delineates plan relationships in conjunction with the vertical treatment of the sides of the rotunda and with stairs and elevations shown connecting the floors. Within the floor plate itself, spatial relationships between enclosed cubicles, fixed elements like bathrooms and enclosed stairs, general work space, and columns are fully revealed by the nature of the view. Between the ceiling and floor plans there is a visual hinge. Above it, the drawing reverses its view, looking up to the ceiling of the typical floor, continuing vertically along the sides of the rotunda, and finally to the intricate steel tracery

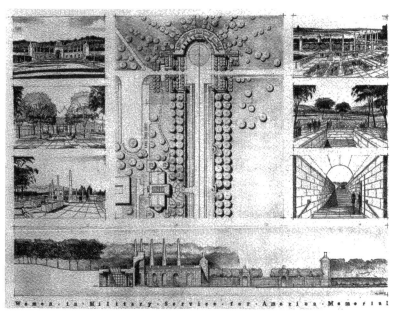

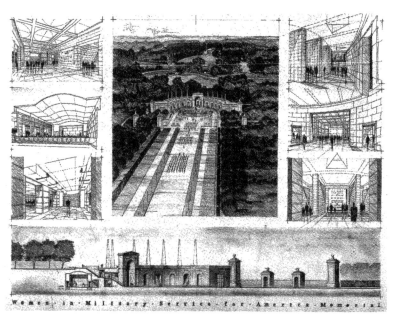

Figure 8.16 Marion Weiss and Michael A. Manfredi (Weiss/Manfredi Architects): Women in Military Service for America Memorial, Washington, D.C., 1989. Plan, sections, perspectives.

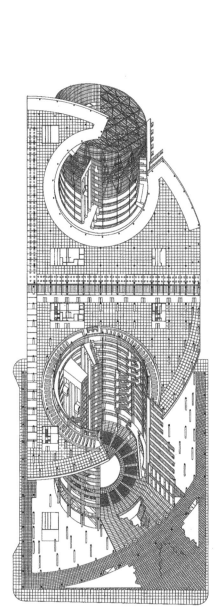

Figure 8.17 Helmut Jahn (Murphy/Jahn): State of Illinois Building, Chicago, Illinois, 1981. Plan oblique, up and down view. Ink, 60″ × 30″.

at the top of the drum. This up view relates ceilings to sides, clarifying the formal relationship of elements. Thus in one succinct drawing, up and down axonometric views clarify horizontal and vertical relationships, viewed in two directions. The drawing quickly summarizes critical formal information while concentrating attention on the central unifying element of the rotunda.

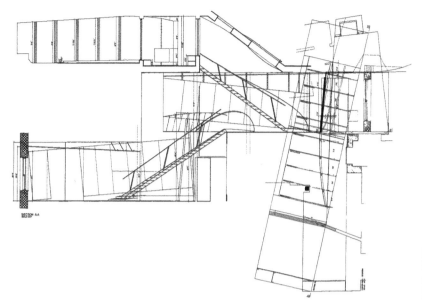

Figure 8.18 Adrian Luchini (Denison Luchini Architects): Cooper Bauer residence, Boston, Massachusetts, 1988. Plan, section. Ink.

In a second example of the use of interconnected drawings, Adrian Luchini's presentation for a loft apartment renovation in Boston superimposes plan, section, and wall elevation (Figure 8.18). He thus focuses attention on the area of overlap and interpenetration. Here in a single drawing, the freestanding mezzanine wall central to the design is represented in plan, section, and in elevation, a single reading yet one which carries with it the imaged information of each separate projection. In the critical zone of the drawing, this wall is marked in section by the thick black, slightly canted line, the base of which is the hinge point common to both the section and plan. He then draws an elevation of the same wall (as revealed by a different section) over the plan and first section. The result is a composite drawing that challenges the viewer's expectations and the conventional manner of reading orthographic drawings. The meticulous precision of the drawing is crucial to maintaining the graphic clarity upon which the unraveling of the layered views depends. As complex as the drawing appears to be, sorting out the compressed and tangled information rewards one with a novel impression of the project, and perhaps even more importantly, a novel sense of the way drawing can model information and stimulate new interpretations.

Presentation drawings are self-conscious propagandistic tools designed to persuade an outside audience. It is precisely this aspect that can result in exaggeration or abuse of drawing as a manipulative tool. The nature of these drawings allows, even encourages, their use for dishonest portrayals, including concealing or minimizing the presence of known weaknesses in a design (by not drawing or by de-emphasizing them), the portrayal of a positive and seductive ambience by focusing on nonarchitectural elements in the drawings, such as glamorous people, lush vegetation, or spectacular sunsets, and the emphasis on qualities in the drawing not necessarily inherent to the project, such as hyperbolized color or texture. The reasons for this self-conscious manipulation include "selling" a weak project, attracting new work, creating fame and recognition, and even marketing the drawings themselves.

The contemporary commodification of drawings has increased awareness of a drawing as a salable artifact. Today almost any drawing by a name designer can be considered a possible commercial product. This is an unfortunate development, as it makes a drawing previously prepared as part of a contemplative and very private condition something which can now be seen as an "art object," a potential commodity. The marketing of drawings has made every drawing, whether preliminary or final, sketch or rendered, a "presentation" drawing.

Many people assume that presentation drawings have nothing to do with design as these are drawings prepared after the fact, merely depicting a finished product. However, presentation drawings also play a critical role in the design process. Their value is not only for their effect on an outside audience. Precisely because of their elaborate and finished aspect, presentation drawings confront their makers as products, as objective evidence lying outside of the cycle of making. The nature of presentation drawings as closure, as finished artifact, causes an author/designer to become part of the external audience, considering the drawing from the standpoint of viewer and critic as well as maker. In this sense, the external orientation of presentation drawings results in an internal effect as well, the viewing by a designer of her or his design through a different viewpoint.

Chapter 9

Visionary Drawings

Giambattista Piranesi brings to life a complex world of labyrinthian space in plate XIV from his series of etchings called the *Carceri* (Figure 9.1). Areas of coarse dark tone alternate with glowing whites; diagonal beams of light enter through mysterious openings above, setting brightness against stark shadows. The drawing is one of excess and reiteration: black against white against black; textured stone piled on textured stone; bridges crossing over bridges; stairs leading to stairs; beams, ropes, and grills abound. Intense, excessive, the drawing is a journey, a wandering, a restless movement deeper and deeper into a labyrinth. After leaving the drawing, one realizes that the labyrinth is still there, continuing in the mind, persistent and haunting:[1]

In the Carceri we have reached a situation where each plate no longer simply represents but is an architectural experience in itself.

Figure 9.1 Giambattista Piranesi: Plate XIV (second state) from the *Carceri*, c. 1750. Perspective. Etching (ink on paper), 16″ × 21½″

Through the most complex system of decoding where conventional perspective sets up expectations only to deny them by introducing fresh patterns, the spectator becomes inescapably involved in the creative process. Each plane embodies a set of endless possibilities (Wilton-Ely 1978, 85).

The *Carceri* demonstrate the potential of a visionary drawing not only to represent the physical form of an environment but also to actively engage a viewer in a mode of perception. An audience is forced to view the world through the representation. Graphic virtuosity, specific qualities of light, point of view, intensity of tone or texture, restlessness or stability of technique, all contribute to the construction of a compelling virtual world.

Drawing offers an unbounded surface for speculative possibilities, and is limited only by graphic technique and imagination. Whether referential, design, diagrammatic, or presentation drawings, they affect manners of seeing, working, and speculating. However, **visionary drawings** push the boundaries of imagination beyond the normative constraints of physicality. The architecture depicted through these drawings is not limited by considerations of gravity, function, scale, or materiality. They conjure, present, and anticipate worlds previously unbuilt and unimagined.[2]

In a sense, all of the drawings included in this chapter could be called presentation drawings, as their intent is to present, to persuade, and to use the rhetorical power of graphics to propagandize an envisioned world. However, they have been included in a separate chapter as a tribute to the tradition of making visionary architecture, to the importance of using drawing as a means to expand exploration, and finally, to the fact that these drawings are wonderful drawings, charismatic, often brooding, full of tone and tenor, powerful and memorable.[3] These are drawings of architecture not imminently intended to be built that depict versions of the future, experienced in the present. Visionary drawings make a new synthetic world of the "base materials of separate worlds, molded by thought's relativity" (Woods 1985, 55).

One of the techniques that Piranesi exploits to create this effect is two-point perspective construction. For example, he uses low vantage points in most of his drawings with the horizon line near (and sometimes at) the base of the plate, forcing one to look up, and thereby emphasizing the height and grand scale of the architecture. Vanishing lines fan up from the horizontal base, becoming increasingly steep diagonals at the top. The bottom thus seems to act as a beginning point, and the top subsequently seems to open out. These lines climb upward and outward, reinforced by light flowing in from above and unbounded by any visible ceiling. The effect is further heightened by the location of vanishing points and station points. Vanishing points are located at approximately equal distances to the left and right. The result is similar angles for the two directions of foreshortening and no visual emphasis for the planes vanishing to the left or to the right. This effect is also reinforced by the many glimpses through walls directed toward one vanishing point which are blocked beyond by walls which vanish toward the other. One plane opens up to the next, juxtaposing the second direction and breaking the continuity of spatial flow.

Piranesi also manipulates the depiction of light freely to exaggerate the spatial effect, casting it from above from ambiguous sources like stage lighting. Is this natural light entering a roofless (or partially roofed) interior? The treatment of shadows suggests the quality of very bright, direct light like natural light: The shadows are shown roughly parallel, suggesting that they could not come from a single, artificial light source (like a lamp), which would cast radiant shadows; there is never any indication of multiple shadows cast by several sources, as would be true for an interior lit by several lamps; the shadows are sharp-edged; and a high level of contrast is used. The indication, in other words, is of a dark, cavernous interior paradoxically illuminated by a bright, strong sun. The pattern of diagonal shadows heightens the formal complexity of counterposed vanishing lines. Ambiguity is further strengthened by the fact that some of the diagonal light lines are aligned with architectural conditions such as the diagonal orientation of stairs.

There is a sense of spatial ambiguity, complexity, and mystery in this plate. It is as if one is not sure how big these spaces are, what the relationship of their elements is, or what the relationship of the viewer to the space is. One of the reasons for this sense of uncertainty is the fact that the frame trims off floor and ceiling planes. The result is that the two planes often used for key depth clues are removed as an indication of the relationship of vertical planes. It is difficult, if not impossible, to locate the walls relative to their base or top. On the right, walls and a bridge structure reiterate the frame by reinforcing its shape.

These elements are rendered darkly, a type of defined boundary which suggests foreground and layered depth.

It is clear that Piranesi has exploited the qualities possible within his chosen mode of representation, two-point perspective. He hyperbolizes its effects through construction techniques, composition, and cropping. He presents a concept of two-point perspective as the drawing construction able to suggest infinite extension or nonclosure. So his *Carceri* represent at once a space of material quality and through its mode of representation an idea about representation itself.

Figure 9.2 Lebbeus Woods: AEON 41, 1985. Perspective. Ink on paper, 30″ × 20″.

Lebbeus Woods opens contemporary windows into worlds related to that of Piranesi's eighteenth century *Carceri*. To be impressed with his masterful draftsmanship is inevitable, and like Piranesi, his graphic virtuosity is a means to project a viewer into the domain of his imagination. Figure 9.2 presents a view looking into a structural matrix of square and circular struts where one cannot be sure of orientation. Woods removes the visual clues which fix directionality. For a moment the viewer may feel suspended precipitously over a bottomless abyss. The next, one seems to be looking up into an infinitely tall shaft. A moment later, one believes one is looking sideways or else the pit reappears. The beam and strut spreaders which tie the walls together (or hold them apart) can be seen as either vertical or horizontal constructs. In one orientation the light seems to be filtering down from above, in the other it is emanating from some glowing source to the side. Woods's quick, sure strokes build up tones of gray, black, and in their absence, white, defining thick dense walls and heavy muscular structures bathed in ambiguously directed light. It is an enigmatic space, powerfully present in the drawing by virtue of his deft rendition of its physical substance, yet disturbing in its quality of being ungrounded. It is at once real and illusive, a vertiginous domain of uncertainty.

In this drawing by Étienne-Louis Boullée of a night view of his project for Newton's Cenotaph (Figure 9.3), light and scale are exaggerated to produce a dramatic, emotional depiction. Its sublime monumentality is heightened by the low and distant perspectival viewpoint and by the inclusion of human figures and rows of trees dwarfed by the building. Through the perspective construction, the building is represented as being far from the viewer, giving one a sense of approaching down a long axis. Boullée described his work as an "architecture of shadows," and it is his use of chiaroscuro in ink wash that distinguishes this and his other graphics (Lemagny 1968, 16). Described as an exterior at night, the bright light coming from the left casts crisply edged shadows. Most notably, there are three crescent-shaped shadows cast by a strong light source to the left. Two are cast by cornices capping both horizontal bases while a third almost identical shape occurs on the left bottom edge of the sphere itself. It is this third shape, an edge of light and darkness, that creates a sense of mystery and enigma, for there is no feature in the building that could cast such a shadow. Instead, darkness is thrown by an unseen and unknown presence. A further puzzling detail occurs. The light source, which splits the dark clouds in the upper right (perhaps the moon?), is

Figure 9.3 Étienne-Louis Boullée: Newton's Cenotaph, exterior by night, 1784. Perspective. Ink and wash, 15⁷⁄₁₆″ × 25⁵⁄₈″. (Courtesy of the Bibliothèque Nationale, Paris, France).

Figure 9.4 Hugh Ferriss: "A City of Needles," 1924.

contradicted by the direction of cast shadows. Dark is set against light, shadows against bright, the light of the stage brought into the frame of a drawing.

Hugh Ferriss renders a powerful vision of a city of widely spaced towers in a drawing illustrating a design for the architect Raymond Hood in 1924 (Figure 9.4). This is a world of slender, 1000–1400-foot-tall towers, spaced over a system of highways where crystalline shapes glow from an unknown light source at the base and darken as they reach toward the glow through the clouds. The darkened sky, gloomy buildings, and blackened silhouettes marching relentlessly to the horizon create an extraordinarily tangible, stark, and disturbing mood. Ferriss believed that an "authentic rendering" needed to depict more than mere physical fact of the architecture and instead must convey its emotional and intellectual experience (Leich 1980, 18). Here is a vision of a world both unbuilt and perhaps unbuildable, an idea given form and heightened through the drama of the drawing.

In a 1919 proposal for an office building in Berlin (Figure 9.5), Mies van der Rohe presents a dramatic polemic on future urbanism: a vision removed from the existing city. Intended for exhibition, it is a highly rhetorical graphic in which Mies depicts the new architecture as shiny, transparent, and light, surrounded by an old neolithic city of dullness, opacity, and darkness. He tones the old buildings almost completely black, leaving just a few flecks of white as remnants of texture in their dull, lifeless surfaces. In contrast, the new building glows with luminous vitality, its taught, sleek transparent skin opening to and revealing a multitiered interior. Mies deftly manipulates his charcoal stick to capture the transparency and reflectivity of glass, and at the same time transport the viewer's imagination to a new (and at that time little-known) world of glass architecture. Earlier versions of this proposal were montages superimposed on photographs, but here Mies uses charcoal to seamlessly bind these two propositions in the same drawing, creating a striking depiction of his vision of the city to come.

Paolo Soleri illustrates his radical responses to the inefficiency of conventional cities by creating drawings of gigantic urbanizations so immense as to defy easy comprehension. In Hexahedron (Figure 9.6), he includes a silhouette of the Empire State Building in the upper right for scalar reference, allowing the viewer to grasp the size of his proposal and the grandiosity of his vision. Soleri renders the new urban configuration with a remarkably fine accretion of surface detail and a high degree of articulation, enhancing the sense of scale of the places within the city. With a wedge-shaped section he cuts the city open to reveal an inner void large enough to contain the Empire State Building. Shade and shadow help to give the city form a place in the sun and to give the inner spaces a sense of openness and closure. The viewer is able to project him or herself into the scene, to stand on balconies and look up (or down) into the vast

Figure 9.5 Mies van der Rohe, Ludwig: Friedrichstrasse Office Building, Berlin. Project, 1921. Perspective. Charcoal and pencil on brown paper mounted to board, 68¼″ × 48″. (Collection, Mies van der Rohe Archive, The Museum of Modern Art, New York. Gift of the architect).

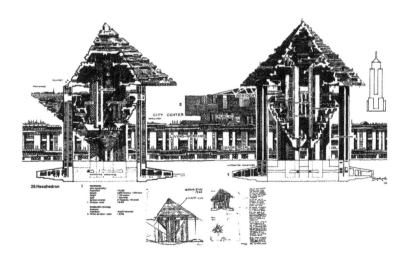

Figure 9.6 Paolo Soleri: Hexahedron (from *Arcology: The City in the Image of Man*), 1969. Section. Ink on paper, 30″ × 36″.

Figure 9.7 Massimo Scolari: "Gateway for a city on the sea," 1979. Oil on paper, 18½″ × 15⁹/₁₆″.

central void, and perhaps even to inhabit the city for a moment. The deep shadows under the pyramidal "roof" give the space the kind of monumentality associated with labyrinths of deep, mysterious spaces.

The drawings of Piranesi, Woods, Boullée, Mies, and Soleri illustrate the use of conventional drawing techniques—albeit in an extremely skillful manner—to draw unconventional architecture. Another type of visionary drawing is the use of drawing itself to speculate on the nature of representation. That is, many drawings are visionary in the sense that they question the nature of architecture by questioning the means that one uses to arrive at it. Representation is questioned and thereby architecture itself.

In an oil painting titled *Gateway for a City on the Sea* (Figure 9.7), Massimo Scolari presents the viewer with a scene that combines two familiar but normally independent forms of three-dimensional representation: perspective and axonometry. Thus Scolari moves the viewer into the realm of enigma, a representation which is about the nature of representation. Perspective dominates this graphic: The waves gradually diminish in size; the building glimpsed through the gate appears distant and reduced through foreshortening; atmospheric perspective has been employed to depict the scene through the gate in colors less saturated and in lighter values than in the foreground; even the clouds seem to diminish perspectively. Yet the gate itself is an enigma, its planar surfaces depicted as parallel lines and surfaces; joint lines do not foreshorten but instead are drawn parallel to each other. As a result, the representational conventions for the gateway are ambiguous: Is the gateway drawn as an axonometric projection and are its lines and surfaces actually parallel and therefore drawn parallel; or, is the gateway depicted perspectively and are the lines which are parallel in the painting actually not parallel in the object itself but rather splay away from each other? In other words, is this a gate in axonometric or perspectival projection? Without knowing the answer, one is not able to know exactly what the gate actually looks like.

By placing a gate depicted evidently in axonometric projection in a scene dominated by perspectival conventions, both methods of representation are called into question. Perhaps the distant structure is not actually distant? The juxtaposition of graphic techniques lifts the gateway from the space of the perspective, suspending it in a moment of uncertainty, allowing

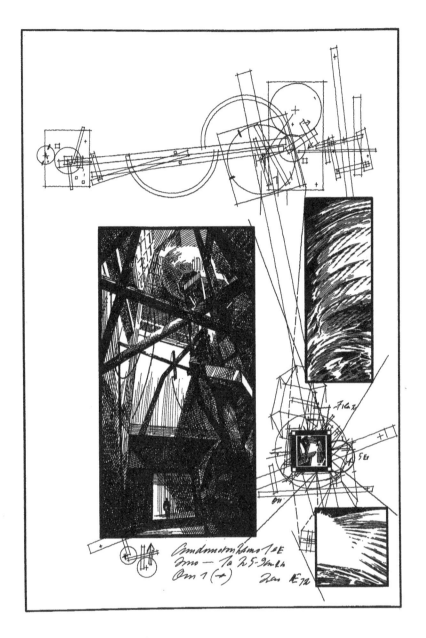

Figure 9.8 Lebbeus Woods: Center for New Technology, Montage 4. Ink on paper, 22½″ × 15″.

one to look through its opening into the space of a new method of viewing architecture. The representation constructs its own viewpoint. If the rules of representation and perception are somehow different in this depicted world, what other strange effects might one encounter or imagine?

In a plate published in his book *Origins* (Figure 9.8), Lebbeus Woods intertwines a series of drawings into an interrelated composition that challenges conventions of representation. Woods joins drawings of indefinite scale, type, and imagery to the familiar drawing construct of a perspective of a room demarcated by a human figure. The perspective describes a tall room, interlaced by struts and beams, with a mysterious stair ascending to a sphere at the top of the space. The view is slightly canted, light streaming in from above, casting richly textured shadows, with an opening from the room to a human figure entering, or leaving, just removed from the reality of the space. Although unusual in proportions, the room seems at least vaguely recognizable and the drawing type identifiable. It is this familiarity that establishes the possibility to be disturbed by the other drawings, for it is this juxtaposition that places the rest of the plate in question. One can speculate that the drawing at the top of the plate is a plan or section, and wonder which of the squares with rectangles is the plan of the room shown. If in fact one part of the drawing above is a plan of the room in perspective, then it is evident that only a small part of the domain has been shown in the perspective and even more perplexing spaces lie beyond. The largest of the "details" on the right might be a detail, might be a kind of microscopic enlargement showing cellular structure, or might be a drawing of the overall structure showing a gargantuan cablelike spiral. They suggest biological qualities and therefore the possibility of enlarged details, and their context is hinted at by connecting lines moving from detail to "plan." However, their context is not known with certainty and one can in fact postulate that the "plan" is a detail of the "detail."

Thus Woods teases with representation, establishing an implied but unfixed relationship between drawings that allows one to assume and project, only to be faced with uncertainty and the sense that one might be misleading oneself. Scale and context remain ambiguous and linking lines can be read from one to another or from another to one. In a final doubt, is it possible that these five drawings are not in fact separate drawings connected to one another but could be only one drawing, making the "perspective" not a drawing of a deep space but a flat graphic pasted on a white wall with inscribed lines? Clues are given, but obscurely; possibilities unfold only to be questioned.

The enigma of Michael Webb's drawing of a "view" of the Regatta Course at Henley-on-Thames (Figure 9.9) carries the viewer far beyond the boundaries of conventional representation. As a composite configuration of marks, words, and tones, it is a graphic investigation and commentary on the premises of perception and representation. The rules of construction are unfamiliar, although an accompanying text, a kind of instruction manual, provides very specific description of the drawing's

Figure 9.9 Michael Webb: "The Landscape Surrounding the Regatta Course, Henley-on-Thames, England," 1992. Altered photograph of layered oil paint on board, 13½″ × 9¼″

parameters: scale (varies by axis), location of observer, weather data, atmospheric density, and explanatory notes. Some recognizable elements suggest possible conventions of construction, such as hints of perspective, cast shadows, and silhouette. Though it is difficult to construe from the image itself, the drawing is in fact an aerial view of a horizontal cut through a one-point eye-level perspective. With its carefully drafted projections and graded tones meticulously built up of layers of oil paint, the drawing in essence depicts a plan view of a cone of vision, affected by atmospheric density and containing white shapes that represent the spaces hidden from view behind solid objects.

In his 1830 watercolor of Sir John Soane's design for the Bank of England (Figure 9.10), Joseph Michael Gandy uses drawing to depict a unique vision, a past of a future, a ruin of a building not yet built.[4] He strips away layers of construction, leaving the left corner intact to establish a context, but in a manner similar

BANK OF ENGLAND with various offices

Figure 9.10 J.M. Gandy: "Bird's-eye view of the Bank of England," 1830. Perspective. Watercolor. (By courtesy of the Trustees of Sir John Soane's Museum.)

to an exploded axonometric, cuts through walls, roofs, and floors, revealing interiors, patterns of rooms, major and minor spaces. The drawing could be considered informational, almost conventional, but for his literal depiction of decomposing masonry and especially for his handling of tone and entourage that charges the drawing with a palpable mood of foreboding and poignancy. Vegetation is shown encroaching from both lower corners, and in the lower right, virtually encrusting mangled remnants. In the upper corners, dark gray wash runs diagonally across both paper and building like clouds or rain, dampening light and darkening mood. This is a vision of an unknown and uncertain time where the future of a building is past, where ruins stand solitary, uninhabited, subject to decay. This is the vision of a master draftsman who has established in the viewer's world a gaze into a past yet to be.

The elaborate, constructed nature of visionary drawings manifest imaginary worlds which cannot exist in any other realm except through drawing. Such drawings represent more than the shapes of an intended object; they evoke a sense of light, atmosphere, monumentality, texture, and intent. In this sense, a drawing represents an author's entire virtual world, nascent in the imagination. Once drawn, this world *is*, it exists, it has presence. Powerful visionary drawings like these are not only representations of architectural intentions, but also presentations of architectural visions which can only be experienced through drawings. By pulling viewers into their world, drawings become experiences to be remembered. They open windows between the immediate physical world and the worlds created by the drawings, evoking experiences of being there, making visions indelible and changing images of the world. Through their graphic charisma, outsiders become insiders, no longer viewers but rather participants in an envisioned world. Having experienced the internal worlds created by these drawings, many are left with a haunting sense of space which persists in the labyrinths of the mind, to be pursued, to be created, to be represented.

Chapter 10

Representation

Escaping this flatland is the essential task of envisioning
information—for all the interesting worlds (physical, biological,
imaginary, human) that we seek to understand are inevitably and
happily multivariate in nature—not flatlands (Tufte 1990, 12).

The author of a drawing attempts to raise a drawing from its
"flatland," pulling the lines from the paper. Yet this is the irony
of drawing, for it is its flatness, its two-dimensionality that is at
once its limit and single greatest advantage. It is this compression
of depth, this concentration of form that makes it the
"multivariate tool" that it is. It is richly varied in the way that
a two-dimensional representation can catalyze a three-dimensional
conception, the manner that a personal drawing can
communicate to others, in its multi-sensual nature, and how it
shapes and is shaped by the intricacies of imagination.

Each drawing type's particular form of editing has virtues and
advantages. Drawings select information in order to clarify
specific modes of seeing. One of their key aspects is the ability
to eliminate and reduce in order to clarify and increase understanding. No drawing is a lesser drawing. A plan is not less than
an axonometric because it concretizes only two rather than three
dimensions. Rather, it is a particular type of effective but
different abstraction allowing an increased potential to see new
possibilities through the filter of a plan view. Each construction
offers similar specific potentialities for organizing perception
and understanding.

In a similar way, each application of drawing has a focus of
intent, concentrating an author's attention on a particular aspect
for a specific reason: Referential drawings represent and structure a way of seeing when studying existing forms; diagrams

serve as formats for analysis and clarification; design drawings are involved with a project's initiation and development; presentation drawings self-consciously persuade through graphic charisma; visionary drawings use the exploratory possibilities of drawing to expand the boundaries of architecture. Architects use drawings as a means for speculation, testing ideas through their graphic representation, each application contributing a way of speculating about architecture in a particular manner.

The experience of drawings is a surprisingly multi-sensual one, involving not only the sight of a mark made but also the tactility of a soft pencil drawn across textured paper, the sound of a pen scratching in a sketchbook, even the smell of ink or paper. Each drawing tool and surface has its own proclivities, engaging in a dialogue of action with the user. Softly shaded tones of gray can be drawn with black ink, but it is a very different drawing process than attempting to achieve the same qualities with a soft pencil. Drawing on the brittle hardness of tracing paper with charcoal like Louis Kahn (Figure 10.1) offers easy possibilities of erasure and transparent grays but makes it difficult to render thin taut lines and crisp edges. Thus a medium has a type of structure with characteristics that foster or inhibit certain inclinations, contributing a unique presence through its graphic personality.

As a technique of drawing circumscribes representation, a drawing itself has a fundamental effect in shaping perception. It acts as a filter for a mode of seeing. The conception of a building formulated first through the perception of a drawing affects the subsequent three-dimensional experience of the building itself. When one has seen the plan of a building, the experience of walking through is altered by its memory. Drawings create their own recall, establishing a conceptual framework of a place, predating and prefiguring perceptions. In a sense, having experienced the drawing first, one views a building relative to its representation.

Completed drawings have their own physical presence and materiality independent of their maker. They confront viewers, even their authors, as objects. In this sense, they are objective evidence of subjective ideas. Drawings stand as representations of imaginary worlds, as virtual images. But they are also things in and of themselves. It is this dichotomy of virtuality and physical reality that allows a designer to overcome the authority of prior ideas by transforming them in reaction to their objectification. In the words of Michael Graves:

Figure 10.1 Louis I. Kahn: Salk Institute Conference Center, La Jolla, California, 1960–61. Site plan, elevations, section. Graphite on yellow trace, 11¾″ × 12½″. (Copyright 1977 Louis I. Kahn Collection, University of Pennsylvania and Pennsylvania Historical and Museum Commission.)

Once we have modeled or represented an idea, that representation, the object made, begins to have a life of its own, somewhat separate from or beyond our original conception. The new life of the physical object then conditions further ideas and thoughts in a process of development . . . I find this interchange between idea and artifact to have the capacity to embrace phenomena outside itself and to allow us to broaden the intensity of the idea through memory and thoughts of things past. The spirit of invention could be said to occur between the reciprocity of thought and object . . . The tension of lines on paper or cardboard in space has an insistence of its own that describes possibilities which perhaps could not be imagined in thought alone (Graves 1981, 38).

Drawing's involvement in the process of thought and representation is not a simple, linear condition of presentation/ representation or conceptualization/drawing but rather one of a complex, interwoven relationship between presentation/ representation, drawing/building/language, and thought. Drawings represent thoughts, giving them visual form, but they then exist as objects in themselves to be viewed and to influence subsequent ideas. If the first idea that led to the first drawing could be called an origin and the drawing a re-presentation, then the second idea that has been developed in response to that first drawing is a re-presentation itself. In this sense, an idea is not always "original," a cause, and a drawing "only" representation, an effect. That is, first, last, cause and effect intertwine in the process of representation. Drawings stir new conceptions through their marks on papers, ideas that exist because of and through the material presence of the drawing act. In this sense, they are both representations and origins, that which comes to be represented through other means.

In this way a few drawings, somehow chosen out of a multitude of sketches, can become a guiding force to a project, acting as a kind of authoritative origin, such as the early conceptual sketch of Le Corbusier for the Carpenter Center (Figure 10.2). That is, this kind of representation guides subsequent actions, their development and representation by future drawings. Key graphics like this, pinned on the wall, published in books, are used in a normative manner, with later drawings judged as to their accuracy in representing the spirit of the "original." In some way, a drawing becomes a critical presence, persistent, often lasting in the mind beyond the construction of the building itself. Even the constructed artifact could then be seen as a

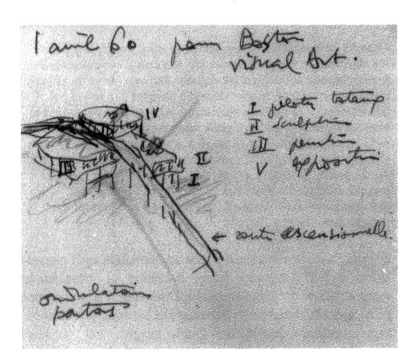

Figure 10.2 Le Corbusier: Carpenter Visual Arts Center, Boston. Conceptual sketch, 1960. Ink, colored pencil. (© 1992 ARS, New York/SPADEM, Paris).

representation of this type of drawing, as an attempt to present again through a three-dimensional medium the power of potential seen originally in two dimensions.

In a manifestation of the idea of a building representing a drawing, Borromini self-consciously used built form rhetorically to represent a drawing concept. In his design of the Palazzo Spada in Rome (Figure 10.3), he exaggerated the effects of foreshortening by tapering its form in both plan and elevation toward a point and by decreasing the spacing of columns toward the end of the colonnade. In a sense, he used three-dimensional built form to represent the nature of perspectival drawing, building in exaggerated foreshortening for rhetorical effect.[1] In a second example of a design representing the effects of perspective (Figure 10.4), Rodolfo Machado and Jorge Silvetti use a deep doorway to frame a view in their hotel project, giving a flattened two-dimensional sense to a three-dimensional view, as if the viewer is looking not at a space but a drawing. The designers attempt to self-consciously represent

Figure 10.3 Borromini: Palazzo Spada, Rome, c. 1652. Plan and perspective. Pencil. (Courtesy of the Graphische Sammlung Albertina, Vienna).

Figure 10.4 Rodolfo Machado and Jorge Silvetti (Machado and Silvetti Associates): Hotel in San Juan Capistrano, California, 1982. Perspective.

the nature of perspectival drawing through built form (Silvetti 1984, 20).

A building can also represent a form of representation other than drawing, for example a model or even a literary text. Peter Eisenman has continually questioned the role of representation in the working process and has self-consciously included ideas about it in his projects, such as House II (Figure 10.5) and more recently House X:

What is the reality of architecture? Is it the actual building, which is detailed and planned to look as if it were made of "nonreal" building material, such as cardboard? Many people see photographs of House II as if they are pictures of the model, rather than the house. Thus, the actual building is, in itself, in one sense, unreal. This, in turn, poses the question, is the cardboard model of the building the reality, or is the ideal of the model and the actual building the reality (Eisenman quoted in Gandelsonas and Morton 1980, 270).

Drawings represent specific architectural conditions such as walls, floors, roofs, and windows, but certain drawings have also come to represent other ideas, acting to crystallize the attitudes or ideals of a specific time and coming to symbolize an architectural viewpoint. They are laden with meaning beyond the representation of particular physical facts. A viewer looks through the drawing to see a representation of a value system, charging the physical artifact with ideas. During the Renaissance, for example, perspective was seen as a symbolic form representative of the humanistic, rationalistic ideals of the period (Figure 10.6). In a similar manner in the 1920's, axonometry was heralded as the drawing construct symbolic of

Figure 10.5 Peter Eisenman: House II, Hardwick, Vermont, 1969. Photograph. (Courtesy of Peter Eisenman, Architect).

a new modern notion of non-hierarchichal, infinite space
(Figure 10.7). Both perspective and axonometry depicted
physical elements but also stood as symbolic forms endowed
with meaning, representing the ideology of their makers. In a
sense, what was drawn was not as important as how it was
drawn, that is, the drawing type itself signified a polemical
position.

These meanings are not constant and inherent to a specific
drawing or drawing type; rather, individuals assign meanings to
drawings, endowing them with particular interpretive structures. For this reason, meanings can be reassigned, removed, or
created anew. Thus perspective as a drawing medium has a very
different resonance for contemporary users than it did during
the Renaissance. During the Renaissance, perspective was a
"discovery," a new method of seeing the world, a medium
charged with significance beyond its ability to represent physi-

Figure 10.6 Central Italian School, late
fifteenth century: "View of an Ideal City."
Perspective. 30″ × 56½″. (Walters Art
Gallery, Baltimore, Maryland).

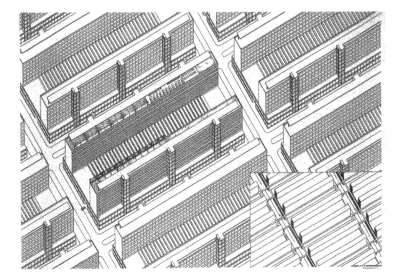

Figure 10.7 Ludwig Karl Hiberseimer,
German (1885–1967): "City Planning
Proposal; Variation Introducing Three
Levels of Traffic." Ink line drawing on
heavy tan paper, 23½″ × 33″. Gift of
George E. Danforth. (Photograph courtesy
of The Art Institute of Chicago).

cality. Today, perspective is an ordinary method of drawing, useful, convenient, and revealing, a tool like a pencil. Its meaning has been altered; its conception changed.

Drawings also exist as a source of information about their authors, as difficult to interpret as verbal evidence but potentially as rich a source of understanding. There are relatively few complete and documented sources, making it difficult to place drawings in the context of a working process. However, close investigative study of an individual's drawings combined with and compared to their verbal and built record often gives surprising insights. In this book, analysis of drawing seeks to provide understanding about the specific individuals involved as well as the making of architecture through drawing in general.

One can look through this final drawing (Figure 10.8) in an attempt to glean information about its author, Alvaro Siza, just as he uses the drawing as a self-referential device. He draws himself drawing himself, using the graphic as a mirror while he looks through the mirror. Siza confronts the dilemma of representation: the distance between its objectivity and his subjectivity, the impossibility of his body entering into the drawing. He attempts to erase the drawing's boundaries, etching lines as if he wants to connect those representing his hand to his hand itself, drawing the mirror of himself drawing, spiraling tighter and tighter into a dilemma of limit, of flatland, and of deepland. In these moments of drawing, Siza and the architects throughout this book ponder questions and challenge reality, setting lines into imaginative motion, finding the worlds of their architecture.

Figure 10.8 Alvaro Siza: "Self Portrait," 1982.

Endnotes

Preface

[1]In the words of Jorge Silvetti referring to the relationship between means and end: "We know that any practice is determined to a considerable degree by its means of production, by the techniques employed and by the nature of the matter that is being elaborated and transformed . . . In that sense we know, as architects, that every element that enters into the production of architecture, in the process, influences and limits its resulting product, from type of pen, pencil, paper, to financial resources, in one way or another and in various degrees." (Silvetti 1984, 11).

[2]As Edward Hill writes: "Drawing turns the creative mind to expose its workings. Drawing discloses the heart of visual thought, coalesces spirit and perception, conjures imagination; drawing is an act of meditation, an exorcism of disorder, a courting of artistic ideas; above all it is the lean instrument of visual formulation and the vortex of artistic sensibility." (Hill 1966, 1).

1 The Lessons of Drawing for Le Corbusier

[1]Le Corbusier's ability to do finished, precise, and journalistically accurate drawings is documented in *The Early Drawings of Charles-Édouard Jeanneret (Le Corbusier) 1902–1908* by Mary Patricia May Sekler. (Sekler 1977). She cites John Ruskin's philosophies and drawings as an important influence in his education.

[2]Michael Graves describes drawings referring to preexisting phenomena as "referential sketches." He calls a referential sketch a "diary or record of an architect's discovery." We have continued to use this term, referential drawings, as we find it most descriptive of this type of drawings. Refer to: Graves 1977. For a more specific critique by Graves of Le Corbusier's referential sketches, refer to his introduction in *Le Corbusier Selected Drawings*. (Graves 1981a).

[3]Jose Luis Sert describes in a book review how Le Corbusier frequently referred back to his sketchbooks, leafing through them to refresh his memory about various sights and past experiences. In this way, he says, Le Corbusier did not begin a new project with a blank page but rather with a store of drawings and inspirations. (Sert 1983).

[4]The history of the development of the design of the Carpenter Center is

documented in great detail in Sekler and Curtis, 1978. An extensive number and variety of drawings are included as well as a description of their use.

[5]In a description of Le Corbusier's working process, Jerzy Soltan writes how he sketched with charcoal, using a deliberately shaky line, drawing lightly, then erasing, changing the line that he had already made. When he reached a configuration that was satisfactory, Le Corbusier would then trace the result in ink. (Soltan 1987, 5–6).

2 Orthographic Drawings

[1]Mies was in the habit of doing innumerable plan studies, some of them with minute changes. (Tegethoff 1985, 17).

[2]Poché refers to a technique where the thickness of a wall, roof or floor is filled in with a color or tone.

[3]Aalto described the importance of drawing to his design process in the following: "I forget the entire mass of problems for a while, after the atmosphere of the job and the innumerable different requirements have sunk into my subconscious. I then move into a method of working which is very much like abstract art, I just draw by instinct, not architectural syntheses, but what are sometimes childlike compositions, and in this way, on this abstract basis, the main idea gradually takes shape, a kind of universal substance which helps me to bring the innumerable contradictory component problems into harmony." (Aalto 1985a, 97).

[4]Mark Hewitt describes the importance of lines to Aalto's draftsmanship and architecture, indicating his fascination with its effects in his drawings: "What is significant is the way in which Aalto's line work builds a figure out of the page. Mature and self-confident draftsmanship coupled with the use of a soft drawing instrument allows him to literally search for answers through line, to make an intuitive search guided and prodded by the informed disposition and superposition of lead upon paper." (Hewitt 1989, 170).

3 Axonometric Drawings

[1]For a discussion of the historical development of axonometry, refer to Massimo Scolari, "Elements for a History of Axonometry." (Scolari 1985).

[2]In his *History of Architecture*, Auguste Choisy (Choisy 1899) used a series of axonometric drawings, including plan oblique up and down views, elevation obliques, and isometrics to depict historical precedents. His name is now connected with the plan oblique up view (or worm's-eye view) due to his frequent and effective use of this drawing type. His drawings depict buildings with detail and ornamentation suppressed, presenting a diagrammatic and abstracted view of the examples. Reyner Banham referred to the influence of these drawings as showing a "logical construct rather than the accidents of appearance" and as "elegant and immediately comprehensible diagrams." (Banham 1983, 25).

[3]Banham observes of Stirling's drawings that they are similar "to the kind of expository mechanical cut-away drawing of complex machinery . . . [which were] intended to make it possible to strip, reassemble, and

above all, understand sophisticated and enigmatic items of machinery." (Banham 1974, 14).

[4]According to Roland Barthes, symbolic forms can have multiple layers of meaning or what he refers to as "orders of signification." In an architectural drawing, its lines signify specific architectural facts such as walls, doors, windows, etc., which Barthes would term its first order of meaning. However, one can see through the lines of a drawing, information first about a building and second about its designer. For example, a drawing can also be interpreted as referring to the underlying ideology of its makers. This latter meaning would be a second order of signification. (Barthes 1987).

[5]This point of view was also embraced by the Dutch architect Theo Van Doesberg, who stated in 1924: The new architecture is formless . . . It rejects schemes a priori and recognizes neither symmetry nor frontality, instead it offers the plastic richness of an all-sided development in space and time." He goes on to explain the inherent unsuitability of perspective drawing for this new architecture as it requires a multiple and non-hierarchichal view rather than the fixed viewpoint of a specific perspective construction. (Van Doesberg quoted in Lampugnani 1982, 12).

4 Perspective Drawings

[1]Bernard Schneider refers to the differences between representations that are oriented to the viewing subject, like perspective drawings, and drawings that are oriented toward the objects being drawn, such as orthographic and axonometric drawings. (Schneider 1981, 81).

[2]In a book review of Arthur Drexler's *The Drawings of Frank Lloyd Wright*, a former student of Wright, Barry Byrne, emphasizes the peripheral role that Wright himself played in the preparation of perspective drawings. Instead he cites the important role of Marion Mahony and other assistants. He also argues that perspectives "played little, if any part in the Wright procedure in design . . . Plan and elevation sufficed, for he planned with a complete sense of three-dimensional qualities." (Byrne 1963, 108). Here we attempt to show how the perspective drawings did in fact play a role, serving as a means to test design changes.

[3]In an account of the beginning of the design, Donald Hoffmann describes the different memories of five apprentices who were with Wright at the time. Their recollections vary from one memory that he drew his ideas on trace within fifteen to twenty minutes to another who thought that he did them early in the morning. (Hoffman 1978, 16).

[4]Wright commonly had apprentices mechanically construct perspective drawings from plans and elevations. He then worked over these constructions, adding color, foliage and detail for drawings presented to clients or making freehand alterations to drawings used within the office for design purposes. In the case of these two drawings, Wright finished them by adding color, trees, foliage, and small details. (Hoffmann 1978).

[5]Although the techniques of perspective construction are methodical and prescribed, in actual practice, drawings are often "adjusted" from the straightforward construction in order to show hidden information or to correct what looks "distorted." That is, constructions are often changed in order to look more "real." The professional delineator Hugh Ferriss

sanctioned these adjustments in his 1926 article on rendering: ". . . the renderer's commission is to depict the building as truthfully and completely as possible in a single drawing. In such a case, it would appear that he is not so much permitted as actually required to slight incidental facts of his viewpoint in favor of the essential facts of the subject which he is viewing." (Ferriss 1926, 148).

[6]It can be argued that the viewpoint or station point of a two point perspective construction is a type of center, but there is no identifiable single visual center or point in the drawing itself like there is in one point construction. In other words, there is a conceptual but not a formal center.

[7]In a seminal article on perspective, Erwin Panofsky discusses perspective as representing "mathematical" rather than "psychophysiological" space. That is, he details how the construction methods of perspective result in idealizations of visual qualities, not vision itself. He further gives examples of how this representation of vision affects vision itself. (Panofsky 1924–25).

[8]Studies of vision indicate that the area of focused vision available to the stationary eye is severely limited. As a result, the eye flicks from one position to another for intervals of less than $1/20$th of a second. (Neisser 1971, 6).

[9]Hans Höllander reiterates the differences between perspective construction and vision: "In fact, however, we are dealing with modes of representation and not modes of seeing . . . From this point of view all methods of representation are correct if their rules are known. Central perspective is a method of representation, and its rules are those of Euclidean geometry, not of psychology or physiology." (Höllander 1984, 77).

5 Referential Drawings

[1]As mentioned in the notes from Chapter 1, we have continued to use the term, referential drawings, as originally suggested by Michael Graves in his article, "The Necessity for Drawing: Tangible Speculation." (Graves 1977). He describes how an author draws from a specific viewpoint, interpreting a preexisting condition through the drawing, thereby allowing the drawer to identify more closely with the subject of the graphic.

[2]Vincent Scully writes of the importance of the drawings that Kahn prepared to record his experiences while travelling, especially the importance of his 1950–51 trip to Italy, Greece, and Egypt, during which he drew Figure 5.1. Scully writes that the drawings from this period prefigure and encapsulate the forms and concerns of his architecture. (Scully and Holman 1978, 10).

[3]Kahn built these drawings like buildings are built, stacking up layers of graphite strokes in a manner similar to masonry courses. "He remarked that he could not draw from the roof down because that was not the way buildings were made. He wanted to reconstruct the process of building by the use of graphite on paper." (Hochstim 1991, 32).

[4]The comparison of Goodhue's and Aalto's drawings is similar to the comparison of medieval and Renaissance drawings by E.H. Gombrich

(Gombrich 1960). He describes how medieval drawings employed deliberately and carefully inscribed figural outlines, meant to be drawn without hesistancy, shakiness or uncertainty. They were ruled lines directed toward a predetermined ideal: the perfect line. This is similar to the finished and carefully controlled nature of Goodhue's drawing. In contrast, the manner of drawing developed during the Renaissance employed a multiplicity of lines, drawn, over-drawn, changed, and corrected. It resulted in a sketch, a drawing of spontaneous nature (the word is derived from the Latin *schedium*, or extemporaneous poem). Because the end figure is not so precisely prefigured, the drawing procedes in an evolutionary manner with lines made in reaction to other lines, as illustrated by Aalto's drawing manner. He marked, and re-marked, in a shifting process of graphic dialogue with the tool.

6 Diagrams

[1]Jorge Silvetti describes the advantages of the reductive process of all representations: "What interests us in all this is that in the process of representation there is a reduction, a loss of some qualities or attributes and then that there is a choice, a preference for others which, by being chosen, occupy 'more space' as it were, the space of the missing attributes, and become more apparent, marked and insightful . . ." (Silvetti 1982, 170). What distinguishes diagrams from other drawings is their degree of reduction, their extreme level of abstracted simplicity.

7 Design Drawings

[1]George Ranalli notes of Scarpa: "His method was to overlay drawing upon drawing until it became so dense that white tempera was then applied to it and he started again on top of it. This method gave the drawing such depth and density that one could almost feel its construction . . . The process is elaborate and develops always in a metaphorical relationship to the built work." (Ranalli 1984, 4).

[2]Marco Frascari describes Scarpa's drawings as manifestations of process and intent, combining a hard-line matrix with freehand doodles. "They are the wonderful calligrams of technological thought, the analogical expression of the processes of construction . . . It is evident that this manner of graphic expression is not based on mimesis of form, but rather it is a procedure for a simulation of an architectural reality." (Frascari 1991, 33).

[3]Michael Graves refers to two stages of preparatory drawings, or early beginning studies, and definitive drawings, or those scaled and precisely drawn. (Graves 1977). In an introduction to *The Architect's Eye*, Robert Stern defines taxonomies of initial sketch, the developed sketch and definitive drawing, and finally the working drawing or construction document. (Nevins and Stern 1979).

[4]In a similar manner Kahn sometimes did figure/ground plan studies, blackening the building mass in order to define it in contrast to the space defined.

[5]Kenneth Frampton describes how Siza inscribes the body in his work: "The author is always there in the unmarked, implied foreground of the delineated image inviting one to oscillate back and forth between subject

and object, between the position of the viewer and that of the imagined, imaginary being or body of the building." (Frampton 1991, 73).

8 Presentation Drawings

[1]We have chosen to use the term presentation drawings because it is the most popularly used term. Other terms include delineations or renderings, developed from the French *rendu,* meaning the "setting down on paper" of an architectural project. (Oechslin 1987, 73).

[2]For a thorough detailing of ink wash techniques as practiced in the École de Beaux Arts, consult *Architectural Rendering in Wash* by H. Van Buren Magonigle (Magonigle, 1922). Magonigle argues for the necessity of learning this technique as ". . . all architecture is merely a matter of light and shade and all draughtsmanship is merely a means by which a man may learn how to distribute his light and shade in beautiful ways." (Magonigle 1922, 95).

[3]During the nineteenth century, architectural competitions played a greater role in the selection of architects for major projects. Because of the pressure to produce compelling (and successful, that is, winning) drawings, a new group of freelance renderers developed, who specialized in the preparation of seductive delineations, especially perspective drawings. (Powell and Leatherbarrow 1983, 29).

[4]For a more complete description of this technique and its development, refer to comments made by Pelli in *Architectural Drawing: The Art and the Process.* (Allen and Oliver 1981, 30).

[5]Rudolph distinguishes between sketches, which to him are a direct connection between the imagination and the concrete, and renderings, which are prepared when ideas have crystallized and are used to present to a client. (Rudolph 1972, 6).

[6]Dawn Ades writes: "By the juxtaposition of elements by nature strange to one another, hallucinatory landscapes are formed; commonplace objects become enigmatic when moved to a new environment. Our thought struggles to encompass them and is baffled or a new thought is made for them. Different realities are thus revealed." (Ades 1976, 19).

[7]In his description of Mies' use of photomontage, Wolf Tegethof describes the landscape in this drawing as taking on a "pictorial, stagelike" character, as if a three-dimensional landscape has been transformed through the representation into a two-dimensional painting. (Tegethof 1985, 128).

[8]Marion Mahony worked in Frank Lloyd Wright's office between 1895 and 1909, and prepared many of the most beautiful drawings to come out of the office. The presentation rendering of this house project in Detroit, the commission of which she inherited from Wright, shows his influence in the design and exhibits many of the graphic techniques she utilized while with him.

9 Visionary Drawings

[1]In the words of Aldous Huxley, the etchings of Piranesi are "metaphysical prisons, whose seat is within the mind, whose walls are made of

nightmare and incomprehension, whose chains are anxiety and their racks a sense of personal and even generic guilt." (Harvey 1979, 8–9).

[2]In his introduction to *The Architect's Eye: American Architectural Drawings from 1799–1978*, Robert Stern refers to Piranesi's drawings as the first "polemical" drawings. He defines these as drawings made without intent of construction, serving rather as a means for speculation. (Nevins and Stern 1979, 21).

[3]Wolfgang Meisenheimer distinguishes between functional and poetic drawings. In a category similar to visionary drawings, he defines poetic graphics as those whose importance is enticing an onlooker and leading them into an untranslatable realm. "They lead into optative landscapes, into discourses of open, 'floating' meaning; they are sustained by the magic of the undefinable. In a word: they are not 'useful' in a narrower sense." (Meisenheimer 1987, 111).

[4]Gandy used architectural drawings "as a medium for historical reflection." (Lukacher 1987, 59).

10 Representation

[1]In this sense it can be said that Borromini represented through built form a quality of perception. In the words of Bernard Schneider: "The visitors to the Scala Regia or the gallery of the Palazzo Spada in Rome are, in a manner of speaking, moving around inside their own eye, experiencing their own perceptual habits and forms of visualization in the 'perspective' structures of a room defined by horizon, eyepoint, and vanishing point. In a very special sense, the experience of architecture is thus transformed into an experience of self. This representational system which is patterned after a form of vision, not only functions as a technical medium; instead it plays the role of the crucial symbolic form of the culture of the times, thus transcending its nature of a means of representation and becoming, in its architectural manifestation, its own subject." (Schneider 1981, 134).

Bibliography

Aalto, Alvar. 1985a. *Alvar Aalto: Sketches*. Edited by Göran Schildt and translated by Stuart Wrede. Cambridge, Mass.: MIT Press.

Aalto, Alvar. 1985b. *Alvar Aalto: Skizzen und Essays*. Vienna: Akademmie der Bildenden Künst.

Achenbach, Sigrid, ed. 1987. *Erich Mendelsohn 1887–1953: Ideen Bauten Projekte*. Berlin: Staatliche Museen Pressischer Kulturbesitz.

Ades, Dawn. 1976. *Photomontage*. New York: Pantheon Books.

Akin, Ömer, and Eleanor F. Weinel, eds. 1982. *Representation and Architecture*. Information Dynamics, Inc.

Allen, Gerald, and Richard Oliver, 1981. *Architectural Drawing: The Art and the Process*. New York: Whitney Library of Design.

Architectural Drawings of the Russian Avant-Garde. 1990. New York: MOMA.

Atkin, William Wilson. 1976. *Architectural Presentation Techniques*. New York: Van Nostrand Reinhold.

Banham, Reyner. 1974. Introduction to *James Stirling* by James Stirling. London: RIBA Publications Ltd.

Banham, Reyner. 1983. *Theory and Design in the First Machine Age*, second edition. London: The Architectural Press, 1960. Reprint. Cambridge, Massachusetts: The MIT Press, 1983.

Barthes, Roland. 1987. *Mythologies*. Translated by Annette Lavers. New York: Hill and Wang.

Berger, John. 1987. "To Take Paper, To Draw: A World Through Lines." *Harper's Magazine* 275 (1648): 57–60.

Blomfield, Reginald, 1912. *Architectural Drawing and Draughtsmen*. London: Cassell & Co., Ltd.

Bois, Yve-Alain. 1981. "Metamorphosis of Axonometry." *Daidalos* 1:40–58.

Böhm, Gottfried. *Das Reichstagsgebäude in Berlin*.

Brooks, H. Allen. 1972. *The Prairie School*. Toronto: University of Toronto Press.

Brooks, H. Allen, ed. 1987. *Le Corbusier*. Princeton, New Jersey: Princeton University Press.

Burns, Howard. 1982. "The Lion's Claw: Palladio's Initial Project Sketches." *Daidalos* 5: 73–80.

Byrne, Barry. 1963. Review of *The Drawings of Frank Lloyd Wright*, by Arthur Drexler. Journal of the Society of Architectural Historians 22 (2): 108–109.

Choisy, Auguste. 1899. *Histoire de l'Architecture*. Paris: Gauthier-Villars, Imprimeur-Libraire.

Clark, Roger, and Michael Pause. 1985. *Precedents in Architecture*. New York: Van Nostrand Reinhold.

Collins, George R. 1968. "The Visionary Tradition in Architecture." *The Metropolitan Museum of Art Bulletin* 26 (8): 310–321.

Collins, George R. 1979. *Visionary Drawings of Architecture and Planning 20th Century through the 1960's*. Cambridge, Massachusetts: The M.I.T. Press.

Crowe, Norman A., and Steven W. Hurtt. 1986. "Visual Notes and the Acquisition of Architectural Knowledge." *JAE* 39 (3): 6–16.

Dal Co, Francesco, and Giuseppe Mazzariol. 1985. *Carlo Scarpa: The Complete Works*. New York: Rizzoli International Publications, Inc.

Descargues, Pierre. 1982. *Perspective: History, Evolution, Techniques*. New York: Van Nostrand Reinhold Company.

Dittmar, Gunter, Kenneth Rogers, and Emmanuel Ginis. 1980. "Architecture and Depiction." *Design Quarterly* 113,114: 4–7.

Drexler, Arthur. 1962. *The Drawings of Frank Lloyd Wright*. New York: Horizon Press.

Drexler, Arthur, ed. 1977. *The Architecture of the École des Beaux-Arts*. New York: MOMA.

Drexler, Arthur, ed. 1986. *The Mies van der Rohe Archive: An Illustrated Catalogue of the Mies van der Rohe Drawings in the Museum of Modern Art*. New York and London: Garland Publishing, Inc.

Dubery, Fred, and John Willats. 1983. *Perspective and Other Drawing Systems*. New York: Van Nostrand Reinhold.

Edgerton, Samuel. 1975. *The Renaissance Rediscovery of Linear Perspective*. New York: Basic Books.

Eisenman, Peter. 1982. *House X*. New York: Rizzoli, 1982.

Fera, Stefano. 1991. "Aldo Rossi: Reelaborations, Journey and Palimpset." *Lotus* 68: 113–121.

Ferriss, Hugh. 1926. "Rendering, Architectural." In *Encyclopedia Brittanica*, 13th edition. London: Encyclopedia Brittanica.

Ferriss, Hugh. 1986. *The Metropolis of Tomorrow*. New York: Ives Washburn, 1929. Reprint. Princeton, New Jersey: Princeton Architectural Press, 1986.

Frampton, Kenneth, and Silvia Kobowski, eds. 1981. *Idea as Model*.

New York: Rizzoli International Publications, Inc.

Frampton, Kenneth. 1991. "Sketching: Alvaro Siza's Notes." *Lotus* 68: 73–87.

Frascari, Marco. 1991. *Monsters of Architecture: Anthropomorphism in Architectural Theory.* Savage, Maryland: Rowman and Littlefield.

Fraser, Iain, and Rod Henmi. 1988a. "The Legacy of Architectural Drawings." In *Architecture and Urbanism: Proceedings of the 75th Annual Meeting of the Association of Collegiate Schools of Architecture.* Washington, D.C.: Association of Collegiate Schools of Architecture.

Fraser, Iain, and Rod Henmi. 1988b. "Visionary Drawing: Memories of the Future." Paper presented at the annual meeting of the Association of Collegiate Schools of Architecture, Miami, March, 1988.

Fraser, Iain, and Rod Henmi. 1991. "From Sketch to Certainty: The Design Drawings of Le Corbusier and Mies van der Rohe." In *Proceedings of the Second International Design Communication Conference,* edited by Warren R. Hampton. Tucson, Arizona: DesignEd Communication Association and the University of Arizona, College of Architecture, Center for Design Communication.

Fraser, Iain, and Rod Henmi. 1992. "The Architect's Mark: One Hundred Years of St. Louis Architectural Drawings." *Gateway Heritage* 12 (3): 46–53.

Futagawa, Yukio, ed. 1985. *Frank Lloyd Wright: Preliminary Studies: 1889–1916.* Tokyo: A.D.A. Edita.

Gandelsonas, Mario, and David Morton. 1980. "On Reading Architecture." In *Signs, Symbols, and Architecture,* by Geoffrey Broadbent, Richard Bunt, Charles Jencks. Chichester, England: John Wiley & Sons.

Gebhard, David, and Deborah Nevins. 1977. *200 Years of American Architectural Drawing.* New York: Whitney Library of Design.

Giurgola, Romaldo, and Jaimini Mehta. 1975. *Louis I. Kahn.* Zürich: Verlag für Architektur.

Glaser, Ludwig, ed. 1969. *Ludwig Mies van der Rohe: Drawings in the Collection of the Museum of Modern Art.* New York: MOMA.

Gombrich, E.H. 1960. *Art and Illusion: A Study in the Psychology of Pictorial Representation.* New York: Pantheon Books.

Goodman, Nelson. 1968. *Languages of Art: An Approach to a Theory of Symbols.* New York: Bobbs-Merrill Co., Inc.

Graves, Michael. 1977. "The Necessity for Drawing: Tangible Speculation." *Architectural Design* 47: 384–93.

Graves, Michael. 1981a. "Le Corbusier's Drawn References." Introduction to *Le Corbusier Selected Drawings* by Le Corbusier. New York: Rizzoli International Publishing, Inc.

Graves, Michael. 1981b. "The Wageman House and the Crooks House." In *Idea as Model,* edited by Kenneth Frampton and Silvia Kolbowski. New York: Rizzoli International Publications, Inc.

Graves, Michael. 1982. "Representation." In *Representation and Architecture*, edited by Ömer Akin and Eleanor F. Weinel. Silver Spring, Maryland: Information Dynamics, Inc.

Gresleri, Giuliano. 1991. "From Diary to Project: Le Corbusier's Carnets 1–6." *Lotus* 68: 7–21.

Guiton, Jacques. 1981. *The Ideas of Le Corbusier on Architecture and Urban Planning*. New York: George Braziller.

Harbeson, John F. 1926. *The Study of Architectural Design: With Special Reference to the Program of the Beaux-Arts Institute of Design*. New York: The Pencil Points Press, Inc.

Harvey, Miranda. 1979. *Piranesi: The Imaginary Views*. London: Academy Editions.

Hewitt, Mark A. 1989. "The Imaginary Mountain: The Significance of Contour in Alvar Aalto's Sketches." *Perspecta* 25: 142–177.

Hill, Edward. 1966. *The Language of Drawing*. Englewood Cliffs, New Jersey: Prentice-Hall, Inc.

Hochstim, Jan. 1991. *The Paintings and Sketches of Louis I. Kahn*. New York: Rizzoli International Publications, Inc.

Hoffmann, Donald. 1978. *Frank Lloyd Wright's Fallingwater: The House and Its History*. New York: Dovers Publications, Inc.

Holl, Steven. 1991. *Anchoring: Steven Holl Selected Projects 1975–1991*. Third Edition. New York: Princeton Architectural Press.

Holländer, Hans. 1984. "On Perspectives." *Daidalos* 11: 71–88.

King, Susan. 1969. *The Drawings of Eric Mendelsohn*. Berkeley: University of California.

Krier, Leon. 1980. *Leon Krier Drawings 1967–1980*. Brussels: Archives d'Architecture Moderne.

Krier, Rob. 1979. *Urban Space*. New York: Rizzoli International Publications, Inc.

Lambert, Susan. 1984. *Drawing: Technique & Purpose*. London: Trefoil Books Ltd.

Lampugnani, Vittorio. 1982. *Architecture of the 20th Century in Drawings: Utopia and Reality*. New York: Rizzoli International Publications, Inc.

Le Corbusier. 1960. *Creation is a Patient Search*. Translated by James Palmer. New York: Frederick Praeger.

Le Corbusier. 1981. *Le Corbusier Selected Drawings*. New York: Rizzoli International Publishing, Inc.

Le Corbusier. 1982. *Le Corbusier Archive*. New York: Garland Publishing, Inc.

Le Corbusier. 1986. *Towards a New Architecture*. Translated by Frederich Etchells. London: J. Rodker, 1931. Reprint. New York: Dover Publications, Inc., 1986.

Leich, Jean. 1980. *Architectural Visions: The Drawings of Hugh Fer-*

riss. New York: Whitney Library of Design.

Lemagny, J.-C. 1968. Introduction to *Visionary Architects*. Houston: University of St. Thomas.

Lissitzky, El. 1970. *Russia: An Architecture for World Revolution*. Translated by Eric Dluhosch. Cambridge, Massachusetts: The MIT Press.

Lukacher, Brian. 1987. "John Soane and his Draughtsman Joseph Michael Gandy." *Daidalos* 25: 51–64.

Magonigle, H. Van Buren. 1922. *Architectural Rendering in Wash*. New York: Charles Scribner's Sons.

Maki, Fumihiko. 1989. *Fragmentary Figures: The Collected Architectural Drawings of Fumihiko Maki*. Translated by Hiroshi Watanabe. Tokyo: Kyuryudo Art Publishing Co., Ltd.

Mauduit, Caroline. 1988. *An Architect in Italy*. New York: Clarkson N. Potter, Inc.

Meier, Richard. 1990a. *Richard Meier*. New York: St. Martin's Press.

Meier, Richard. 1990b. *Richard Meier: Building for Art*. Basel, Switzerland: Birkhäuser Verlag.

Meier, Richard. 1991. *Richard Meier 1985/1991*. New York: Rizzoli International Publications, Inc.

Meisenheimer, Wolfgang. 1987. "The Functional and the Poetic Drawing." *Daidalos* 25: 11–120.

Meyers, Marshall D. 1987. "Louis Kahn and the Act of Drawing: Some Recollections." In *The Louis I. Kahn Archive: Personal Drawings*, edited by Alexander Tzonis. New York: Garland Publishing, Inc.

Mies van der Rohe, Ludwig. 1986–90. *The Mies van der Rohe Archive*. New York: Garland Publishing, Inc.

Moschini, Francesco, ed. 1980. *Massimo Scolari: Watercolors and Drawings 1965–1980*. New York: Rizzoli International Publications, Inc.

Murphy, Richard. 1990. *Carlo Scarpa and the Castelvecchio*. London: Butterworth Architecture.

Neisser, Uric. 1971. "The Processes of Vision." In *Perception: Mechanisms and Models*, with introductions by Richard Held and Whitmand Richards. San Francisco: W. H. Freeman and Company.

Nevins, Deborah, and Robert Stern. 1979. *The Architect's Eye: American Architectural Drawings from 1799–1978*. New York: Pantheon Books.

Nooteboom, Cees. 1985. *Unbuilt Netherlands: Visionary Projects by Berlage, Oud, Duiker, Van den Broek, Van Eyck, Hertzberger and others*. New York: Rizzoli International Publications, Inc.

Oechslin, Werner. 1982. "The Well-Tempered Sketch." *Daidalos* 5: 99–112.

Oechslin, Werner. 1987. "Rendering'—The Representative and Expressive Function of Architectural Drawings." *Daidalos* 25: 68–77.

Panofsky, Erwin. 1924–25."Perspective as Symbolic Form." Translated from Vorträge der Bibliothek Warburg. New York: New York Institute of Fine Arts, New York University.

Pauly, Daniéle. 1987. "The Chapel of Ronchamp as an Example of Le Corbusier's Creative Process." Translated by Stephen Sartarelli. In *Le Corbusier*, edited by H. Allen Brooks. Princeton, New Jersey: Princeton University Press.

Pehnt, Wolfgang. 1985. *Expressionist Architecture in Drawings*. New York: Van Nostrand Reinhold.

Pei, I.M. 1978. *I.M. Pei & Partners Drawings for the East Building, National Gallery of Art: Its Evolution in Sketches, Renderings, and Models 1968–1978*. Washington, D.C.: Adams Davidson Galleries.

Pelli, Cesar. 1990. *Cesar Pelli: Buildings and Projects 1965–1990*. New York: Rizzoli International Publications, Inc.

Pfeiffer, Bruce Brooks. 1990. *Frank Lloyd Wright Drawings: Masterworks from the Frank Lloyd Wright Archives*. New York: Harry N. Abrams, Inc.

Pierce, James Smith. 1967. "Architectural Drawings and the Intent of the Architect." *Art Journal* 27: 48–58.

Portoghesi, Pado. 1968. *Borromini*. London: Thames & Hudson.

Powell, Helen, and David Leatherbarrow. 1983. *Masterpieces of Architectural Drawing*. New York: Abbeville Press.

Ragghianti, Carlo Ludovico. 1978. "Alvar Aalto's Creative Imagination." In *Alvar Aalto 1898–1976*, edited by Aarno Ruusuvuori. Helsinki: Museum of Finnish Architecture.

Ranalli, George. 1984. Introduction to *Drawings for the Brion Family Cemetery* by Carlo Scarpa. New Haven, Connecticut: Yale School of Architecture.

Reidemeister, Andreas. 1982. "The Sketch as a Practical Instrument." *Daidalos* 5: 26–34.

Robbins, Edward. 1988. "Drawing and the Social Production of Architecture." *In The Design Professions and the Built Environment*, edited by Paul L. Knox. New York: Nichols Publishing Company.

Rossi, Aldo, 1983. *Aldo Rossi Galerie-Edition*. Zürich: Jamileh Weber Galerie.

Rowe, Colin, and Fred Koetter. 1978. *Collage City*. Cambridge, Massachusetts: The MIT Press.

Rudolph, Paul. 1972. *Paul Rudolph: Architectural Drawings*. New York: Architectural Book Publishing Company.

Ruskin, John. 1900. *The Elements of Drawing: in Three Letters to Beginners*. London: George Allen.

Scarpa, Carlo. 1984. *Drawings for the Brion Family Cemetery*. New Haven, Connecticut: Yale School of Architecture.

Schildt, Göran. 1967. *The Sculptures of Alvar Aalto*. Helsinki: The Otava Publishing Co.

Schildt, Göran, ed. 1985. *Alvar Aalto: Sketches*. Cambridge, Massachusetts: The MIT Press.

Schildt, Göran. 1991. "The Travels of Alvar Aalto: Notebook Sketches." *Lotus* 68: 35–47.

Schneider, Bernhard. 1981. "Perspective Refers to the Viewer, Axonometry Refers to the Object." *Daidalos* 1: 81–95.

Scolari, Massimo. 1985. "Elements for a History of Axonometry." *Architectural Design* 55 (5–6): 73–78.

Scolari, Massimo. 1987. *Hypnos*. New York: Rizzoli International Publications, Inc.

Scully, Vincent, and William G. Holman. 1978. *The Travel Sketches of Louis I. Kahn*. Philadelphia: Pennsylvania Academy of the Fine Arts.

Scully, Vincent. 1991. "Marvelous Fountainheads. Louis I. Kahn: Travel Drawings." *Lotus* 68:49–63.

Seitz, William C. 1961. *The Art of Assemblage*. New York: MOMA.

Sekler, Eduard F., and William J.R. Curtis. 1978. *Le Corbusier at Work: The Genesis of the Carpenter Center for the Visual Arts*. Cambridge: Harvard University Press.

Sekler, Mary Patricia May. 1977. *The Early Drawings of Charles-Edouard Jeanneret (Le Corbusier) 1902–1908*. New York: Garland Publishing, Inc.

Sert, Jose Luis. 1983. "A Key to Understanding Le Corbusier." *AIA Journal* 70 (11): 67–69.

Silvetti, Jorge. 1982. "Representation and Creativity in Architecture." In *Representation and Architecture*, edited by Ömer Akin and Eleanor F. Weinel. Silver Spring, Maryland, Inc.: Information Dynamics, Inc.

Silvetti, Jorge. 1984. "Perspective and the Envious Longing for the Renaissance." *Daidalos* 11: 10–21.

Siza, Alvaro. 1988. *Travel Sketches*. Porto, Portugal: Documentos de Arquitectura.

Siza, Alvaro. 1990. *Alvaro Siza: Architectures 1980–1990*. Paris: Centre Georges Pompidou.

Soleri, Paolo. 1969. *Arcology: The City in the Image of Man*. Cambridge, Massachusetts: The MIT Press.

Soleri, Paolo. 1971. *The Sketchbooks of Paolo Soleri*. Cambridge, Massachusetts: The MIT Press.

Soleri, Paolo. 1975. *Arcology and the Future of Man*. Montgomery, Alabama: Montgomery Museum of Fine Arts.

Solomon, Barbara Stauffacher. 1988. *Green Architecture and the Agrarian Garden*. New York: Rizzoli International Publications, Inc.

Soltan, Jerzy. 1987. "Working with Le Corbusier." In *Le Corbusier*, edited by H. Allen Brooks. Princeton, New Jersey: Princeton University Press.

Spiers, Richard Phene. 1888. *Architectural Drawing*. New York: Cassell & Co., Ltd.

Stirling, James. 1974. *James Stirling*. London: RIBA Publications Ltd.

Stirling, James. 1982. *James Stirling*. New York: Academy Editions/St. Martin's Press.

Stirling, James, and Michael Wilford and Associates. 1984. *James Stirling: Buildings and Projects*. New York: Rizzoli International Publications, Inc.

Stirling, James. 1991. Letter to authors, October 7, 1991.

Takamatsu, Shin. 1988. *The Killing Moon and Other Projects*. London: The Architectural Association.

Tegethoff, Wolf. 1985. *Mies van der Rohe: The Villas and Country Houses*. New York: MOMA.

Tufte, Edward R. 1990. *Envisioning Information*. Cheshire, Connecticut: Graphics Press.

Tzonis, Alexander, ed. 1987. *The Louis I. Kahn Archive: Personal Drawings*. New York: Garland Publishing, Inc.

Van Zanten, David T. 1966. "The Early Work of Marion Mahony Griffin." *The Prairie School Review III* (2): 5–23.

Visionary Architects. 1968. Houston: University of St. Thomas.

Walton, Paul H. 1972. *The Drawings of John Ruskin*. Oxford: Clarendon Press.

Wang, Wilfried, ed. 1988. *Alvaro Siza: Figures and Configurations. Buildings and Projects 1986–1988*. New York: Rizzoli International Publications, Inc.

Webb, Michael. 1987. *Temple Island: A Study of Michael Webb*. London: Architectural Association.

Whitaker, Charles Harris, ed. 1925. *Bertram Grosvenor Goodhue– Architect and Master of Many Arts*. New York: Press of the American Institute of Architects, 1925. Reprint. New York: Da Capo Press, 1976.

White, John. 1967. *The Birth and Rebirth of Pictorial Space*, 2nd edition. London: Faber.

Whittick, Arnold. 1956. *Eric Mendelsohn*. London: Leonard Hill Ltd.

Willis, Carol. 1987. "Unparalleled Perspectives: The Drawings by Hugh Ferriss" *Daidalos* 25: 78–91.

Wilton-Ely, John. 1978. *The Mind and Art of Giovanni Battista Piranesi*. London: Thames and Hudson.

Woods, Lebbeus. 1978. *Centricity: The Unified Urban Field*. Berlin: Galerie für Architektur und Raum.

Woods, Lebbeus. 1985. *Origins*. London: The Architectural Association.

Woods, Lebbeus. 1989. *OneFiveFour*. New York: Princeton Architectural Press.

Woods, Lebbeus. 1991. *Lebbeus Woods: Terra Nova*. Tokyo: a + u Publishing Co., Ltd.

Zakníc, Ivan, ed. and trans. 1987. *Le Corbusier: Journey to the East*. Cambridge, Massachusetts: The MIT Press.

Zevi, Bruno. 1970. *Erich Mendelsohn Opera completa: Architetture e Immagini Architettoniche*. Milan: ETAS/KOMPASS.

Zoelly, Pierre. 1991. *A Journey to Turkey: Architectural Notes*. Basel, Switzerland: Birkhäuser Verlag.

A

Aalto, Alvar, 39–41, 92–95
Acropolis, Athens:
    Kahn, 82–83
    Predock, 84–85
Administration Building of the German
    Metalworkers (Mendelsohn), 71–72
American Heritage Center and Art
    Museum, Univ. of Wyoming
    (Predock), 125–29
Angkor Wat, Cambodia (Pelton), 90, 91
Architect in Italy (Mauduit), 88–89
Architectural office, St. Louis (Bricken),
    51–52
"Architecture and Pangeometry"
    (Lizzitsky), 53–54
Atmospheric perspective, 138
Avery Coonley house, Riverside, Illinois
    (Wright), 63–65
Axes of measurement:
    axonometric drawings, 56
    orthographic drawings, 42
Axonometric drawings, 45–57
    axes for measurement, 56
    Bricken, William, 51–52
    dimensions, 46
    down view/up view, 48, 57
    elevation oblique drawing, 47
    exploded view, 52–53
    Holl, Steven, 52–53
    isometrics, 57
    James Stirling, Michael Wilford and
        Associates, 47–50, 55
    Lizzitsky, El, 53–54
    obliques, 57
    plan oblique view, 47–48
    Vinciarelli, Lauretta, 46–47
    Wilke, Ulrike, 50–51

B

Banco Pinto & Sottomayor, Oliveira de
    Azemeis (Siza), 124
Berkowitz House, Martha's Vineyard
    (Holl), 52–53
Bibiena, Ferdinando Galli, 75–76
"Bird's-eye view of the Bank of England"
    (Gandy), 157–58
Bohm, Gottfried, 31–32, 33
Borromini, 165–66
Boullee, Etienne-Louis, 151–52, 154
Bricken, William, 51–52
Brion Cemetery, San Vito Altivole, Italy
    (Scarpa), 113–16
Brise soleil, 18

C

Calascibetta, Italy (Aalto), 92–94
Carceri (Piranesi), 147–48, 150, 151
Cast shadows, 31
Center for New Technology, Montage 4
    (Woods), 155–56
Central Italian School (fifteenth century),
    167
Cheney House (Wright), 29–30
Childe Harold Wills house (Mahony),
    142–43

City Hall and Central Library of The Hague, Netherlands (Richard Meier and Partners), 30, 32

"City of Needles, A" (Ferriss), 152

"City Planning Proposal: Variation Introducing Three Levels of Traffic" (Hiberseimer), 167

Clark, Roger, 101

Collage City (Rowe/Koetter), 107–8

Combined views, 34–36

Comparative plan diagrams (Roger Clark/Michael Pause), 101

Conceptual drawings, 115

Cooper Bauer residence (Luchini), 145

Copper, Wayne, 107–8

Corea, Mario, 119–21

Covered swimming pool, Badalona, Spain (Corea), 119–20, 121

Cranbrook School, Bloomfield Hills, Michigan (Eliel Saarinen), 77, 134–35

D

Design drawings, 113–29
    and architectural study, 114
    Corea, Mario, 119–21
    Kahn, Louis, 116–19
    Le Corbusier, 6, 114
    phases of, 115
    Predock, Antoine, 125–29
    Scarpa, Carlo, 113–16
    Siza, Alvaro, 120–24

Diagrams, 99–111
    defined, 99–100

"Draftsman drawing a portrait, A" (Durer), 78

Drawing applications, 81–168
    design drawings, 113–29
    diagrams, 99–111
    presentation drawings, 131–46
    referential drawings, 82–97
    representation, 161–68
    visionary drawings, 147–50

"Drawing of a stage design" (Bibiena), 75–76

Drawing types, 23–79
    axonometric drawings, 45–57
    orthographic drawings, 25–43
    perspective drawings, 59–79

Durer, Albrecht, 78

E

Eisenman, Peter, 99–100, 166

Electra Bookstore (Stirling), 48

Elevation, 34

Elevation oblique drawing, 47

Engineering Laboratories at Leicester, England (Stirling), 47–48

F

Fallingwater, *See* Kaufmann House

Ferriss, Hugh, 133–34, 152

Fiske, Bradford, 34, 35

Floor plans, 26–30

Fogg Museum New Building (Stirling), 49–50

Fragmentary Figures (Maki), 36

Francesca, Piero della, 74–75

Fraser, Iain, 95, 97

Friedrichstrasse Office Building, Berlin (Mies van der Rohe), 152–53

Fuente, Julian de la, 11

Fujisawa Gymnasium (Maki), 36–37

G

Gandy, Joseph Michael, 157–58

Gateway for a City on the Sea (Scolari), 154–55

Gilbert, Cass, 132–33

Goodhue, Bertram, 92, 94

Graves, Michael, 162–63

Great Hall at Principia College
        (Maybeck), 32, 33
Gropius, Walter, 109–10

H

Hardline developmental drawings, 115
Henmi, Rod, 95, 96
Hexahedron (Soleri), 153–54
Hiberseimer, Ludwig Karl, 167
Hockney, David, 45
Holl, Steven, 52–53, 55
Hotel Danieli, Venice (Maki), 87–88
Hotel project (Machado and Silvetti
        Associates), 165–66
House II, 166
Hubbe House (Mies van der Rohe), 70–71
Hurricane, Cape Cod, Massachusetts
        (Aalto), 95

I

Ideogram, 12
Imperial Hotel, Tokyo, Japan (Wright), 66
Isometrics, 57
Isozaki, Arata, 105–6

J

Jahn, Helmut, 104–5, 143–44
James Stirling, Michael Wilford and
        Associates, 47–50, 55
Jeanneret, Charles-Eduoard, *See* Le
        Corbusier
Jefferson National Expansion Memorial
        Competition, St. Louis, Missouri
        (Eero Saarinen), 137–38

K

Kahn, Louis, 30, 31, 32, 34, 82–83, 91,
        116–19, 162

Kaufmann House, Mill Run, Pennsylvania
        (Wright), 62–63, 66–69, 132
Kimbell Museum, Fort Worth, Texas
        (Kahn), 32, 34, 116–17, 119
Kirin Plaza Building, Osaka, Japan
        (Takamatsu), 34
Koetter, Fred, 107–8
Krier, Leon, 109
Krier, Rob, 108

L

Le Corbusier:
    brise soleil, 18
    design drawings, 6
    design process, 8–9
    drawings, 1–21
        Carpenter Visual Arts Center, 9–21,
            164–165
        Chapel at Ronchamp (France), 7–8
        cow with calf, 2, 3, 10
        pyramid and sphinx, 4
        rural church, 7
        view from airplane, 3–4, 10
        view of ship's promenade, 4–5
        Villa Adriana at Tivoli, 5–6
    ondulatoires, use of, 10, 18
    presentation drawings, 14–18
    referential drawings, 5
    sketchbooks, 1–2, 6–8
Le Petit Trianon (Shank), 90, 91
Lizzitsky, El, 53–54
Long Gallery House (Pelli), 34, 35
Luchini, Adrian, 145

M

Machado, Rodolfo, 165–66
Mackey, Eugene Jr., 86–87
Mahony, Marion, 142–43
Maison Carre, Bazoches, France (Aalto),
        39–41
Maki, Fumihiko, 36–39, 87–88
Manfredi, Michael A., 143–44

Marfa II project (Vinciarelli), 46–47

Mauduit, Caroline, 88–89

Maybeck, Bernard, 32, 33

Medici Chapel, Florence (Mackey), 86–87

Mendelsohn, Eric, 71–72, 94

Metz House, Staten Island (Holl), 52

Mies van der Rohe, Ludwig, 26–29, 70–71, 141, 152–53, 154

Montenventoso, Italy (Goodhue), 92, 94

Museum for the Decorative Arts, Frankfurt am Main, Germany (Richard Meier & Partners), 103–5, 139

Museum of Modern Art, Gunma, Japan (Isozaki), 105–6

Museum for Northrhine Westphalia, Dusseldorf (Stirling), 48–49

Museum of Scotland project (Wilke), 50–51

N

National Capitol, Dacca, Bangladesh (Kahn), 30, 31

National Life Insurance Company Office Building (Wright), 59–61

National Museum of Western Art (Henmi), 95, 96

"New Goa" (Siza), 122, 123

Newton's Cenotaph (Boullee), 151–52

O

Obliques, 57

Origins (Woods), 155

"Orthogonal Plans for Squares" (Rob Krier), 108

Orthographic drawings, 25–43
  Aalto, Alvar, 39–41
  axes of measurement, 42
  Bohm, Gottfried, 31–32
  combined views, 34–36
  dimensions, 46

elevation, 34, 43
Fiske, Bradford, 34, 35
floor plans, 26–30
as generators, 43
Kahn, Louis, 30, 31, 32, 34
Maki, Fumihiko, 36–39
Maybeck, Bernard, 32, 33
Mies van der Rohe, Ludwig, 26–29
Pelli, Cesar, 34, 35
Richard Meier and Partners, 30, 32
sections, 31–32
site plans, 30–31
site sections, 32
Takamatsu, Shin, 34
Wright, Frank Lloyd, 29–30

P

Palazzo dei Banchi, Bologna, Italy (Mauduit), 88–89

Palazzo Spada (Borromini), 165–66

"Parallel of Cities, the Human Dimension" (Leon Krier), 109

Pause, Michael, 101

Pelli, Cesar, 34, 35, 135–36, 140

Pelton, Jane, 90, 91

Perspective drawings, 59–79
  aerial views, 63–65, 67
  angle of view relative to object surfaces, 78
  Bibiena, Ferdinando Galli, 75–76
  eye-level views, 63–64, 67
  Francesca, Piero della, 74–75
  interior views, 63, 65–66
  Mendelsohn, Eric, 71–72, 94
  Mies van der Rohe, Ludwig, 70–71
  one-point perspective, 74–75, 79
  plan projection, 78
  Rudolph, Paul, 72–73
  section perspective, 72–74
  Silvetti, Jorge, 74–75
  thumbnail drawings, 65–66, 103
  two-point perspective, 75–76, 79
  Wright, Frank Lloyd, 59–69

Piranesi, Giambattista, 147–51, 154
Precedents of Architecture (Clark/Pause), 101
Precise definitive drawings, 115
Predock, Antoine, 84–85, 125–29
Presentation drawings, 131–46
    design drawings compared to, 131
    Ferriss, Hugh, 133–34
    Gilbert, Cass, 132–33
    Jahn, Helmut, 143–44
    Le Corbusier, 14–18
    Luchini, Adrian, 145
    Mahony, Marion, 142–43
    Mies van der Rohe, Ludwig, 141
    Pelli, Cesar, 135–36, 140
    Richard Meier & Partners, 139
    Rudolph, Paul, 138–39
    Saarinen, Eero, 137–38
    Saarinen, Eliel, 134–35
    Takamatsu, Shin, 136–37
    Weiss/Manfredi Architects, 143–44
    Wright, Frank Lloyd, 141–42
"Proposal for Downtown Redevelopment," St. Louis, Missouri (Ferriss), 133–34
Prospecti of an Ideal City (Francesca), 74–75

R

"Rayon in L.C. mother's house" (Siza), 122, 123
Referential drawings, 82–97
    Aalto, Alvar, 92–95
    defined, 82
    double phenomenon presented by, 86
    Kahn, Louis, 82–83
    Le Corbusier, 5
    Mackey, Eugene Jr., 86–87
    Maki, Fumihiko, 87–88
    Mauduit, Caroline, 88–89
    Predock, Antoine, 84–85
Regatta Course at Henley-on-Thames (Webb), 156–57
Reichstafsgebaude, Berlin (Bohm), 31–32, 33

Representation, 161–68
    drawing types, form of editing, 161
    drawing's involvement in, 163
    of specific architectural conditions, 166
Resor House project, Wyoming (Mies van der Rohe), 141
Richard Meier & Partners, 30, 32, 101–5, 139
Rowe, Colin, 107–8
Royal Dutch Paper Mills Headquarters Building (Richard Meier and Partners), 101–3
Rudolph, Paul, 72–73, 138–39

S

Saarinen, Eero, 137–38
Saarinen, Eliel, 77, 134–35
Saifukuji Buddhist Temple, Japan (Takamatsu), 136–37
Saint Louis Art Museum (Gilbert), 132–33
Salk Institute Conference Center, La Jolla, California (Kahn), 118–19, 163
Salk Institute for Biological Studies, La Jolla, California (Kahn), 117–18
San Gimignano, Italy, street (Kahn), 91
Scaled freehand drawings, 115
Scarpa, Carlo, 113–16
Scolari, Massimo, 154–55
Sections, 31–32
Self-portrait (Siza), 168–69
Shank, Isadore, 90, 91
Silvetti, Jorge, 74–75, 165–66
Site plans, 30–31
Site sections, 32
Siza, Alvaro, 120–24, 168–69
Sketchbooks, Le Corbusier, 1–2, 6–8
Sky Hook (Lizzitsky), 53–54
Small dune (Mendelsohn), 94
Soleri, Paolo, 153–54
State of Illinois Building (Jahn), 104–5, 143–44
Station point, 61

T

Takamatsu, Shin, 34, 136–37
Teachers' Training College, Setubal, Portugal (Siza), 123
Tepia Science Pavilion, Tokyo (Maki), 37–38
Thomas Hardy house (Wright), 142
Thomas Jefferson Library, Univ. of Va., 106–7
Thumbnail drawings, 65–66, 103
Tomb at Bellefontaine Cemetary (Fraser), 95, 97
Towards a New Architecture (Le Corbusier), 2, 25
"Traffic Studies, Center City, Philadelphia" (Kahn), 110–11
Transformational diagrams (Eisenman), 99–100
Turandot stage set (Hockney), 45

U

Ulrich Lange House plan studies (Mies van der Rohe), 26–29

V

Venice Biennal family house proposal (Pelli), 140
"View of an Ideal City" 167
Vinciarelli, Lauretta, 46–47

Visionary drawings, 147–50

Boullee, Etienne-Louis, 151–52, 154
defined, 148
Ferriss, Hugh, 152
Gandy, Joseph Michael, 157–58
Mies van der Rohe, Ludwig, 152–53, 154
Piranesi, Giambattista, 147–51, 154
Scolari, Massimo, 154–55
Soleri, Paolo, 153–54
Webb, Michael, 156–57
Woods, Lebbeus, 150–51, 154, 155–56

W

Ward Willits house (Wright), 141–42
Webb, Michael, 156–57
Weiss/Manfredi Architects, 143–44
Weiss, Marion, 143–44
Wilke, Ulrike, 50–51
Women in Military Service for America Memorial (Weiss/Manfredi), 143–44
Woods, Lebbeus, 150–51, 154
World Financial Center (Pelli), 135–36
Wright, Frank Lloyd, 29–30, 59–69, 132, 141–42

Y

Yale School of Architecture (Rudolph), 72–73
Yale University married student housing project (Rudolph), 138–39